Routledge Library Editions

ESSAYS IN THE THEORY OF ECONOMIC FLUCTUATIONS

ECONOMICS

Routledge Library Editions — Economics

KEYNESIAN &
POST-KEYNESIAN ECONOMICS
In 11 Volumes

ESSAYS IN THE THEORY OF ECONOMIC FLUCTUATIONS

MICHAL KALECKI

Routledge
Taylor & Francis Group

LONDON AND NEW YORK

First published in 1939

Reprinted in 2003 by
Routledge
2 Park Square, Milton Park, Abingdon, Oxon OX14 4RN

Transferred to Digital Printing 2004

Routledge is an imprint of the Taylor & Francis Group

Printed and Bound in Great Britain

British Library Cataloguing in Publication Data
A CIP catalogue record for this book
is available from the British Library

Essays in the Theory of Economic Fluctuations
ISBN 13: 9780415434652

Miniset: Keynesian & Post-Keynesian Economics

Series: Routledge Library Editions – Economics

Printed and bound by Antony Rowe Ltd, Eastbourne

ESSAYS IN THE THEORY
OF ECONOMIC FLUCTUATIONS

by

MICHAL KALECKI

London
GEORGE ALLEN & UNWIN LTD

FIRST PUBLISHED IN 1939

FOREWORD

THESE essays, though formally independent, nevertheless constitute a whole. Each of them treats a problem which is interesting in itself, but at the same time it prepares the ground for the succeeding essays. In particular the first five essays lead up to the sixth, which contains a theory of the business cycle.

The following are reprinted (all with important alterations) by permission of the editors concerned: "The Distribution of the National Income," from *Econometrica*, April 1938, "The Principle of Increasing Risk," from *Economica*, November 1937, and "A Theory of the Business Cycle," from the *Review of Economic Studies*, February 1937.

I am very much indebted to Mrs. Joan Robinson, whose comments have enabled me to make various improvements, and to Mr. Brian Tew for improving the style. I have also to thank Mr. P. Sraffa and Mr. R. F. Kahn for valuable remarks.

CAMBRIDGE,
June 1938

M. KALECKI

CONTENTS

Part One

Part Two

Part One

1

THE DISTRIBUTION OF THE NATIONAL INCOME[1]

INTRODUCTION

In this essay we investigate both statistically and analytically the relative share of manual labour in the national income. From the social point of view it would be more interesting to consider the share of labour as a whole: but it is the relative share of *manual* labour which is suitable for theoretical analysis.

For the same reason the national income is here given a slightly unorthodox meaning. First, as we are interested in the *home produced* income alone, we exclude from national income that part which is derived from foreign investments. Further, we shall deal with *gross* income, by which is meant the income before deductions for maintenance and depreciation (gross income = net income + maintenance and depreciation).[2]

It is easy to see that the gross national home-produced

[1] This essay is an altered version of the article published in *Econometrica*, April 1938. The statistical data differ from those quoted in this article owing either to the slightly altered meaning of some concepts (e.g. of the national income) or to new sources becoming available.

[2] For the sake of brevity we shall speak throughout the essay of "depreciation" instead of "maintenance and depreciation."

income is equal to the value added by all industries of an economy. Usually the Government[1] is treated as an "industry" producing public services, but we shall not adopt this procedure here. Instead we shall mean by national income *the total value added by private enterprises* which we denote below by A.

THE STATISTICAL DATA

1. The figures for Great Britain are based on Professor Bowley's *Wages and Income in the United Kingdom since 1860*, and Mr. Colin Clark's *National Income and Outlay*.

Using Professor Bowley's data on the distribution of national income (pp. 92, 139) and deducting from the total income the income from overseas (mentioned on p. 96) we obtain the relative share of manual labour[2] in home-produced income: 41·4 per cent in 1880, and 39·4 in 1913. These figures are for relative shares in *net* income; Professor Bowley does not give data on depreciation and gross income. The rate of increase of gross income in the period, 1880–1913, is, however, unlikely to differ much from that of net income; for the proportion of depreciation to net income in 1913 was only about 8 per cent, and the changes in the volume of capital equipment and in the national income between 1880 and 1913 were such that this percentage could not have undergone a great proportionate change

[1] We mean here by the Government all public authorities.
[2] Shop assistants excluded.

within this period.[1] Thus the relative share of manual labour in gross income must have altered within the period in question similarly to that in net income. Professor Bowley's figures of national income contain also the value of Governmental services, which should strictly be excluded for our present purpose, but this would for similar reasons only slightly alter the trend of the relative shares of manual labour from 1880 to 1913.[2] Thus it can be concluded from the above that the change in the relative share of manual labour in the national income in our sense (value added by private enterprises) was small.

The figures for 1911 and 1924–35 are obtained from Mr. Colin Clark's data on "Distribution of Income between Factors of Production, 1911 and 1924–35" (*National Income and Outlay*, p. 94), and on depreciation (pp. 86, 169), and expenditure on Governmental services (p. 141) in these years. The relative shares here calculated differ from those given by Mr. Clark (p. 94) in that they are taken in relation to *gross* home-produced income, from which expenditure on public services has been excluded.

---

[1] The real capital per head increased by about 25 per cent, the real income per head by about 40 per cent (*National Income and Outlay*, pp. 273 and 232), while the rate of depreciation was probably to some extent higher in 1913 than in 1880.

[2] The proportionate rise in expenditure on administration army, navy, etc., in Great Britain in the period considered was not much different from that in national income. See, e.g., Bernard Mallet, *British Budgets, 1887–1913*, pp. 353 and 407.

TABLE 1

Relative Share of Manual Labour[1] in the National Income of Great Britain

1911	40·7	1924	43·0	1928	43·0	1932	43·0
		1925	40·8	1929	42·4	1933	42·7
		1926	42·0	1930	41·1	1934	42·0
		1927	43·0	1931	43·7	1935	41·8

We see that the relative share of manual labour in the national income in Great Britain showed a remarkable stability both in the long run and in the short period.

2. The figures for the U.S.A. are based on Dr. King's *The National Income and Its Purchasing Power, 1909–1928*, and Dr. Kuznets' *National Income and Capital Formation, 1919–1935*.

The relative share of wages[2] in the net national income[3] was, according to Dr. King, 37·9 per cent in 1909 and 40·2 in 1925. The change in the relative share of manual labour in the gross income less "Government produced" services was probably not very different.

For the period 1919–34 Dr. Kuznets' estimates are used. It is easy here to calculate "national income" in our sense. We take "income produced" by private industries including depreciation and maintenance (pp. 14, 80). A difficulty arises, however, in connection with wages being estimated separately only in "selected

---

[1] Shop assistants excluded.   [2] Shop assistants included.

[3] *The National Income*, p. 74. We have excluded from income the services of durable consumption goods which King treats as a part of national income (he calls this part "imputed income").

industries": agriculture, mining, manufacturing, construction, and railways; for other industries they are given jointly with salaries (pp. 62–67).

In 1925 the wage bill in the "selected industries" mentioned above was $17 milliards, while the total wage and salary bill (excluding Governmental employees) was about $44 milliards. But according to Dr. King's estimate the wage bill in trade, services, etc., amounted in 1925 to about $13 milliards, so that if we admit his figure we obtain: wages in "selected industries" 17, in other industries 13, and total salaries $14 milliards. Now as regards the amplitude of fluctuations, the wages in "other industries" keep the middle position between wages in "selected industries" and total salaries. Thus they are likely to fluctuate more or less proportionately to the total wage and salary bill. With this hypothesis it is possible to estimate roughly the wage bill in "other industries" throughout the period considered. Adding the results to the wage bill in "selected industries" as given by Dr. Kuznets, we obtain the hypothetical total wage bill in the period 1919–34 and find its relative share in the national income. The figures obtained are given in the following table.

TABLE 2

Relative Share of Manual Labour[1] in the National Income of U.S.A.

1919	34·9	1923	39·3	1927	37·0	1931	34·9
1920	37·4	1924	37·6	1928	35·8	1932	36·0
1921	35·0	1925	37·1	1929	36·1	1933	37·2
1922	37·0	1926	36·7	1930	35·0	1934	35·8

[1] Shop assistants included.

These figures represent of course only a rough estimate, but they are adequate in order to show the stability of the relative share of manual labour in the period considered.

We see that in the U.S.A., as in Great Britain, the relative share of wages in the national income shows but small variations both in the long run and in the short period. We shall now try to explain this "law," and to establish the conditions under which it is valid.

THE DEGREE OF MONOPOLY AND THE DISTRIBUTION OF THE PRODUCT OF INDUSTRY

1. Let us consider an enterprise with a given capital equipment which produces at a given moment an output x and sells it at a price p.[1]

If we denote the entrepreneurial income (inclusive of dividends) per unit of output by e_a, the average "overhead" costs (interest, depreciation, and salaries) by o_a and the average wage and raw material cost by w_a and r_a respectively, we have:

$$p = e_a + o_a + w_a + r_a$$

Further, the short-period marginal costs m (i.e. the cost of producing an additional unit of product with a given capital equipment) is made up of the sum of the short-period marginal cost of "overheads" o_m, wages w_m, and raw materials r_m.

$$m = o_m + w_m + r_m$$

[1] We mean here by p the "net price," i.e. the revenue per unit of product after deduction of advertising costs, etc.

We subtract the second equation from the first and obtain:

$$p - m = e_a + (o_a - o_m) + (w_a - w_m) + (r_a - r_m) \quad . \quad (1)$$

Following Mr. Lerner,[1] we shall call the "degree of monopoly" of the enterprise, the ratio of the difference between price and marginal cost to price, or:

$$\mu = \frac{p - m}{p}$$

If marginal cost is equal to marginal revenue, μ is equal to the inverse of the elasticity of demand for the product of the enterprise. Substituting μ for $\frac{p - m}{p}$ in the equation (1), and multiplying both sides by the output x we get:

$$xp\mu = xe_a + x(o_a - o_m) + x(w_a - w_m) + x(r_a - r_m).$$

Such an equation can be written for each enterprise of an economy. Adding the equations for all enterprises we obtain:

$$\Sigma xp\mu = \Sigma xe_a + \Sigma x(o_a - o_m) \\ + \Sigma x(w_a - w_m) + \Sigma x(r_a - r_m) \quad . \quad (2)$$

The sum Σxe_a is the aggregate entrepreneurial income (inclusive of dividends). Further, the marginal "overhead" cost is in general small in comparison with the

---

[1] "The Concept of Monopoly and the Measurement of Monopoly Power," *Review of Economic Studies*, June 1934.

average cost; thus $\Sigma x(o_a - o_m)$ can be represented by $(1 - \beta)\,O$, where O is the aggregate overhead cost (interest, depreciation, and salaries), and β a small positive fraction. The average cost of raw materials can be supposed approximately constant and consequently the sum $\Sigma x(r_a - r_m)$ can be neglected. Most complicated are the problems connected with the member $\Sigma x(w_a - w_m)$; we must deal with them at some length.

2. The prevailing type of average wage-cost curve seems to have the following shape. It is more or less horizontal up to a point corresponding to the "practical capacity" of the plant, but slopes sharply upwards beyond it. This point is seldom reached—factories, e.g. only exceptionally work in more than two shifts. Thus in enterprises of this type $w_a - w_m$ is small in comparison with w_a.

Of course in some industries the situation is different. Those producing basic raw materials (agriculture and mining) are normally subject to diminishing returns, and $w_a - w_m$ is usually negative and not small as compared with w_a in the enterprises concerned. Other industries have, on the other hand, distinctly falling average wage-costs until "practical capacity" is reached (e.g. railways), and here $w_a - w_m$ is positive and not small in relation to w_a.

It is now easy to see that if wage-cost curves of the first type represent a large part of the aggregate wage bill W the sum $\Sigma x(w_a - w_m)$ is likely to be small in comparison with W. For then in most enterprises $\dfrac{w_a - w_m}{w_a}$

will be small while the rest will be divided between those in which $\dfrac{w_a - w_m}{w_a}$ is positive and those in which it is negative.

We therefore conclude that $\Sigma x(w_a - w_m)$ can be represented by γW where γ is likely to be a small (positive or negative) fraction. In other words: conditions of approximately constant returns prevail, in the short period, in the economy as a whole.

3. On the basis of the above considerations we can now write the equation (2) as follows:

$$\Sigma x p \mu = E + (1 - \beta)O + \gamma W$$

or:

$$\Sigma x p \mu = (E + O) - (\beta O - \gamma W)$$

where β and γ are small fractions.

It is obvious that βO is small in relation to $E + O$; and the same can be said of γW since, as the statistical data quoted above show, W is less than half the gross national income A and thus less than $A - W = E + O$. We can conclude that $\beta O - \gamma W$ is small in comparison with $E + O$, and therefore:

$$\Sigma x p \mu = E + O$$

can be regarded as a good approximation. Now let us divide both sides of this equation by the aggregate turnover $T = \Sigma x p$.

$$\frac{\Sigma x p \mu}{\Sigma x p} = \frac{E + O}{T}$$

The expression on the left-hand side of this equation is the weighted average of the degrees of monopoly μ, which we shall denote by $\bar{\mu}$. The sum $E + O$ is made up of profits, interest, depreciation, and salaries, and thus it is equal to gross capitalist income plus salaries.

We have thus the following proposition: *The relative share of gross capitalist income and salaries in the aggregate turnover is with great approximation equal to the average degree of monopoly:*

$$\bar{\mu} = \frac{E + O}{T} \qquad \cdots \cdots \quad (3)$$

Some remarks are still necessary on the notion of the turnover T. In our above argument by "enterprise" was really meant not the firm but a unit producing marketable goods, e.g. a spinning and weaving mill which belong to the same firm must be considered separate "enterprises." Indeed, such a weaving mill in its pricing would account the yarn from its "own" spinning mill at the market price, and consequently the formation of prices is here much as it would be if the two factories belonged to distinct firms.

Now it is important to stress that with this definition of an "enterprise" the turnover T is *not* dependent on the degree of integration of industry so long as markets for intermediate products are in existence. T is equal to the gross national income plus the aggregate cost of marketable raw materials.

HOW IS IT POSSIBLE FOR THE DEGREE OF MONOPOLY TO DETERMINE THE DISTRIBUTION OF THE PRODUCT OF INDUSTRY?

1. The results obtained in the last section may seem paradoxical. In the case of free competition the average degree of monopoly $\bar{\mu}$ is equal to zero; thus equation (3) seems to show that free competition makes it impossible not only to earn profits and interest, but even to cover depreciation and salaries—all gross income being absorbed by wages. This paradox is, however, only apparent. The formula (3) can be correct only when the assumptions on which it is based are fulfilled. According to these assumptions: (1) The short-period marginal-cost curve does not differ considerably in the majority of enterprises from the short-period average-cost curve of manual labour and raw materials up to a certain point corresponding to "practical capacity." (2) The output in these enterprises is usually below this point. These assumptions are quite realistic, but such a state of affairs is possible only with the existence of monopoly or imperfect competition. If free competition prevails, the second condition cannot be fulfilled; enterprises must close down or maintain such a degree of employment that the marginal cost is higher than the average cost of manual labour and raw materials.

In the real world an enterprise is seldom employed beyond the "practical capacity," a fact which is therefore a demonstration of general market imperfection and widespread monopolies or oligopolies. Our formula though quite realistic is not applicable in the case of free competition.

The second question which may be raised is of a more complex character. According to our formula, the distribution of the product of industry is at every moment determined by the degree of monopoly. Our formula therefore holds both for the short period and in the long run, even though it was deduced on the basis of, so to speak, pure short-period considerations. And contrary to the usual view neither inventions nor the elasticity of substitution between capital and labour have any influence on the distribution of income.

The source of the conflict between our theory and the orthodox view may be explained thus: (1) The long-period analysis of distribution is generally conducted on the basis of oversimplified representation of output as a function of only two variables—capital (taken *in abstracto*) and labour. In this way, the short-period cost curves are, as we shall see at once, excluded artificially from this analysis. (2) On the basis of our assumptions these curves have a special shape which makes for the elimination of factors other than the degree of monopoly from the mechanism of distribution. To clarify the problems concerned we shall now consider the dependence of the long-run distribution of the product of industry on the shape of the short-period cost curves.

2. A particular commodity can be produced with various types of equipment requiring more or less labour and raw materials per unit of product. (A change in the scale of plant is also considered a variation in the

type of equipment.) The conditions of production are, however, determined not only by the choice of the type of equipment, but also by the intensity with which it is used. Not only may the kind of machinery be varied, but it is also possible, for example, to work with the same machinery in either one or two shifts.

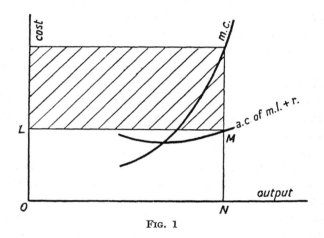

FIG. 1

Let us assume for a moment free competition and draw for each alternative type of equipment which can be applied in the production of the commodity considered a short-period marginal-cost curve and a short-period average-cost curve of manual labour and raw materials (Fig. 1). The shaded area then represents the value of net capitalist's income, depreciation, and salaries, while the unshaded area LMNO represents the cost of manual labour and raw materials.

To determine the position of long-period equilibrium we define first for each type of equipment the level of prices at which the shaded area covers salaries, depreciation, interest, and normal profit (i.e., the rate of profit at which the industry in question neither expands nor contracts). We shall call this price the normal price attached to a given type of equipment, and the corresponding use of this equipment, its normal use.[1] We choose of all types of equipment that to which the lowest normal price is attached. It is easy to see that the normal use of this type of equipment represents the long-run equilibrium. It is clear now that the shape of the short-period marginal-cost curves corresponding to various types of equipment influences the formation of long-run equilibrium.

If some change in basic data takes place, e.g. the rate of interest alters or a new invention occurs, the long-run equilibrium is shifted; a new type of equipment is used in a "normal" way, and in general the relation of the shaded and unshaded areas will be different from that in the initial position. This is quite in accordance with the prevailing long-run theory of distribution. We shall see, however, that such is not the case with the peculiar shape of marginal-cost curves assumed in the deduction of formula (3), and if we admit, instead of free competition, a certain given degree of monopoly.

We take for granted that the short-period marginal-cost curve does not differ appreciably from the average-

---

[1] It is easy to see that with free competition the normal use coincides with the so-called "optimum" use.

cost curve of manual labour and raw materials, below the point A (Fig. 2). We represent them therefore by the same thick curve PMB.

With a given degree of monopoly the relation of price to marginal cost is a constant $\dfrac{1}{1-\mu}$. Thus if output remains below OA the price corresponding to it

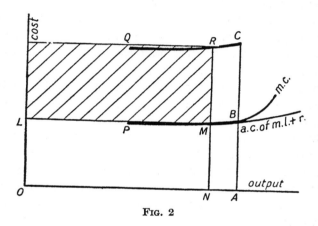

FIG. 2

is represented by the curve QRC, whose ordinates are proportionate to those of the curve PMB. The ratio of the shaded area, representing profits, interest, depreciation, and salaries, to the unshaded area, representing wages and the cost of raw materials, is equal to $\dfrac{1}{1-\mu}$. We define in exactly the same way as before the normal use for each type of equipment as that at which normal profit is earned. The long-run equilibrium is again

27

represented by the normal use of such a type of equipment that, with a given degree of monopoly, it is impossible to earn profits higher than normal by employing a different type. If the basic data alter the new long-run equilibrium is represented by the normal use of a different type of equipment. The long-run equilibrium price of the product alters too, but not its relation to the average cost of manual labour and raw materials, because for all types of equipment the marginal-cost curve coincides with the average-cost curve of manual labour and raw materials, and the degree of monopoly is supposed to be given. In this way the distribution of the product among factors, as expressed by the relation of the shaded to the unshaded area, remains unaffected by changes of basic data so long as the degree of monopoly is unaltered and the use of equipment in the long-run equilibrium does not reach the point A.[1]

The change of basic data may of course influence the degree of monopoly. For instance, technical progress by affecting the size of enterprises influences the degree of monopoly in an industry. In this case such changes influence the distribution of income, but this is not in

---

[1] It may be asked how is it possible for surplus capacity to exist in the long-run equilibrium without inducing firms to curtail their plant. The answer is that large-scale economies prevent the firms from reducing their plant below a certain limit, a state of affairs described by those writers who have shown that imperfect competition must cause equipment in the long run to be used below the "optimum point." See, e.g., R. F. Harrod, "Doctrines of Imperfect Competition," *The Quarterly Journal of Economics*, May 1934.

contradiction with our results, because it is via the degree of monopoly that the influence operates.

THE DISTRIBUTION OF THE NATIONAL INCOME

1. Our aim in this essay is to investigate the changes of the relative share of the wage bill W in the national income A. The difference $A - W$ is of course equal to the sum of gross capitalist's income and salaries. Thus the equation (3) can be written as

$$\frac{A - W}{T} = \bar{\mu} \quad . \quad . \quad . \quad . \quad (3a)$$

In multiplying both sides by $\dfrac{T}{W}$ we obtain

$$\frac{A - W}{W} = \bar{\mu} \cdot \frac{T}{W}$$

From this it follows that the relative share of manual labour in the national income is:

$$\frac{W}{A} = \frac{1}{1 + \bar{\mu} \cdot \dfrac{T}{W}} \quad . \quad . \quad . \quad . \quad (4)$$

This formula shows at once that the increase in the degree of monopoly reduces the relative share of manual labour. The expression increases not only because of the rise in $\bar{\mu}$, but also because $\dfrac{T}{W}$ is increased by a rise in the degree of monopoly since this raises prices in relation to wages.

2. Changes in $\dfrac{T}{W}$ can, of course, be caused by influences

29

other than changes in the degree of monopoly. A change in the price of "basic raw materials," i.e. of the products of agriculture and mining, in relation to wage-costs in other industries, will clearly also have an important influence. It is easy to see that a rise in the prices of "basic raw materials" in relation to wage-cost must result in an increase of *all* prices in relation to wage-cost and consequently in an increase of $\frac{T}{W}$. On the other hand, $\frac{T}{W}$ increases in a much lesser proportion than do "basic raw materials" prices relative to wage-costs. For in each stage of production prices increase (with a given degree of monopoly) proportionately to the sum of raw material- *and wage-costs.*

It is obvious from the formula (4) that with a given degree of monopoly the relative share of manual labour falls when $\frac{T}{W}$ increases, consequently a rise in the prices of "basic raw materials" as compared with wage-costs by raising $\frac{T}{W}$ must lower the relative share of manual labour. (This may be seen also directly from formula (3a) according to which non-wage earners' income $A - W$ changes with a given degree of monopoly proportionately to the turnover T. Thus if the ratio of turnover to wage-bill $\frac{T}{W}$ increases owing to a rise in the prices of basic raw materials as compared with wage-costs, $\frac{A - W}{W}$ must also increase.)

30

It has been noticed already that a rise in the prices of "basic raw materials" relative to wage-costs causes an increase of $\frac{T}{W}$ in a *much lesser* proportion. It is easy to see from formula (4) that the proportionate fall in the relative share of manual labour in the national income is even smaller.

3. We have seen that: (1) A rise of the degree of monopoly causes a decrease in the relative share of manual labour $\frac{W}{A}$. (2) A rise of prices in "basic raw materials" in relation to wage-cost causes a fall in $\frac{W}{A}$ but in a much lesser proportion. We thus have here some reasons for the tendency of the relative share of manual labour in the national income towards stability. For the degree of monopoly does not undergo violent changes either in the long run or in the short period. The fluctuations in the prices of "basic raw materials" in relation to wage-costs, though strong, are as stated above only slightly reflected by changes in manual labour's relative share. But of course if the most unfavourable case of joint action of these factors occurs, the change in manual labour's relative share may be appreciable. We shall see below that the remarkable stability of the relative share of manual labour which we notice in statistics is the result of these determinants working in opposite directions. This phenomenon occurred only by chance during the long period considered, and may cease in the future; but in the business cycle there seems to be a steady tendency for the conflict

31

of these two forces to keep the fluctuations in relative share of manual labour within narrow limits.

CHANGES IN THE DISTRIBUTION OF THE NATIONAL INCOME IN THE LONG RUN

1. The increasing concentration of industry tends undoubtedly to raise the degree of monopoly in the long run. Many branches of industry become "oligopolistic," and oligopolies are often transformed into cartels.

This tendency for the degree of monopoly to increase in the long run may, however, be offset by the diminishing imperfection of the market caused by the fall of transport costs in relation to prices, the standardization of goods, the organization of commodity exchanges, etc. In the *Spaetkapitalismus*, however, the first tendency has the upper hand, and the degree of monopoly tends to increase.

As concerns the secular trend of the relation of the prices of "basic raw materials" to wage-cost, it is difficult to say anything definite *a priori*.

2. As we have seen in the first section the relative share of manual labour in the national income in Great Britain did not change appreciably between 1880 and 1913. It can be shown that the relation of the prices of "basic raw materials" to wage-costs also did not alter in this period. For this purpose we shall compare Sauerbeck's index of wholesale prices with Mr. Clark's index for the deflation of national income.[1] It is clear

[1] *National Income and Outlay*, p. 231.

that the influence of raw material prices as compared with that of wage-costs is much greater upon the first index than upon the second. Now between 1880 and 1913 both of these indices changed in the same proportion (increased by 6 per cent), so that we can conclude that the prices of "basic raw materials" relative to wage-cost did not change. Obviously, then, the degree of monopoly could not have undergone a substantial change between 1880 and 1913 since with raw material prices unaltered as compared with wage-costs such a change would have been reflected in the relative share of manual labour in the national income.

Turning to the period 1913 to 1935, Sauerbeck's index fell during that time by 2 per cent while "income prices" rose by about 60 per cent,[1] which shows that there was a considerable fall in the prices of raw materials in relation to wage-costs. Thus since the relative share of manual labour was stationary between 1913 and 1935, this means that the degree of monopoly must have substantially increased in this period. Had a fall in the prices of basic raw materials not occurred in the last twenty-five years the relative share of manual labour would have tended to fall appreciably and the recent economic and political development of Great Britain would have been quite different.

The course of events in the U.S.A. between 1909 and 1925 was similar. The relative share of manual labour was approximately stable. The wholesale all-commodity

[1] *National Income and Outlay*, pp. 235 and 204.

33   c

index increased in this period by about 50 per cent; King's index of "income prices" by about 80 per cent.[1] Thus here again the degree of monopoly must have risen considerably, but its influence on the relative share of manual labour was counterbalanced by the fall of the prices of "basic raw materials" in relation to wage-cost. It is, of course, not at all certain that in the future the rise in the degree of monopoly will continue to be compensated by a fall in the prices of "basic raw materials." If it is not, the relative share of manual labour will tend to decline.

CHANGES IN THE DISTRIBUTION OF THE NATIONAL INCOME DURING THE BUSINESS CYCLE

1. We shall here examine first the cyclical changes in the prices of "basic raw materials" in relation to wage-cost.

The prices of the produce of agriculture and mining fluctuate much more violently than does the cost of labour in other industries. This is due to the fact that marginal-cost curves in agriculture and mining, as distinct from other sectors of the economy, slope steeply upwards. In addition, wages fluctuate much more in agriculture than in other industries during the business cycle. Consequently "basic raw material" prices rise relative to wage-cost in the boom and fall in the slump.

[1] *National Income and its Purchasing Power*, pp. 74 and 77.

34

Much more complicated is the question of the change of degree of monopoly during the trade cycle. It has recently been argued by Mr. Harrod that the degree of monopoly increases in the boom and falls in the slump. In the slump consumers "resent and resist the curtailment of their wonted pleasures. . . . Their efforts to find cheapness become strenuous and eager. Nor are commercial firms exempt from this influence upon their purchase policy; they, too, have received a nasty jolt and must strain every nerve to reduce costs."[1] Thus the imperfection of the market is reduced and the degree of monopoly diminished.

Mr. Harrod was rightly criticized in that there exist other factors which influence the degree of monopoly in the opposite direction. For instance, in the slump, cartels are created to save profits,[2] and this, of course, increases the degree of monopoly, but when trade revives they are dissolved because of improving prospects of independent activity and the emergence of outsiders.

More important still is the fact that in spite of the fall of prices of raw materials and wages some prices of finished goods tend to be relatively "sticky" in the slump; this for various reasons: entrepreneurs avoid price cuts because it may induce their competitors to do likewise; cartels are not afraid that outsiders will appear, etc. It can be stated on the basis of data quoted

[1] *The Trade Cycle*, pp. 86–87.

[2] Joan Robinson, review of R. F. Harrod, *The Trade Cycle*, *Economic Journal*, December 1936.

above that the influence of these factors in raising the degree of monopoly during the slump is stronger than that of the diminishing imperfection of the market.

Indeed, if we look at our data on the relative share of manual labour in the national income we see that in general it does not change much during the business cycle. But the prices of basic raw materials fall in the slump and rise in the boom as compared with wages, and this tends to raise the relative share of manual labour in the slump and reduce it in the boom. If the relative share of manual labour remains more or less constant it can be concluded that the degree of monopoly tends to increase in the depression and decline in the boom.

We now see that, as has already been mentioned, the apparent stability of manual labour's relative share during the cycle is in reality the effect of the opposite changes in the degree of monopoly and in the relation of the prices of basic raw materials to wages.

2. The stability of the relative share of the wage bill W in the national income A in the short period has far-reaching consequences as regards the formation of the prices of finished goods. Let us divide in the equation:

$$\frac{W}{A} = \text{const.}$$

both the numerator and the denominator of the left-hand side by an index of the volume of output of finished goods. Since the money value of the latter is the national income A we obtain:

THE DISTRIBUTION OF THE NATIONAL INCOME

$$\frac{\text{index of average wage-costs}}{\text{index of the prices of finished home-produced goods}^1} = \text{const.} \quad . \quad (5)$$

Now, as stated above, conditions of approximately constant returns prevail in the short period in the economy as a whole. Thus the index of the average cost of manual labour does not depend appreciably on the level of output and employment and with a constant technique and intensity of work does not differ much from the index of wage rates. Consequently the equation (5) shows that with constant technique and intensity of work prices of finished home-produced commodities change approximately in the same proportion as wage rates. This result clearly is of great importance for the theory of real wages, and will be dealt with in more detail and supported statistically in the essay on "Money and Real Wages." We now propose to apply it to the problem of the prices of investment and consumption goods.

3. Let us consider in an economy the sections which produce consumption and investment goods respectively (including in each the corresponding raw material production). Since our argument throughout the essay is not confined to a closed system the formula (5) applies approximately to each of these two sections. Thus if the technique of production and the intensity of work are unaltered, it may be concluded that the prices of con-

---

[1] All exported commodities must be here included in "finished" goods. Further "prices" are here, strictly speaking, differences between the actual prices of commodities and the cost of foreign raw materials used in their fabrication.

sumption goods will move proportionately to wage rates in consumption goods industries. A similar development may be supposed to take place in the investment goods industries. It therefore follows that the ratio of the price indices of finished investment and consumption goods $\frac{p_i}{p_c}$ is in the short period approximately equal to the ratio of indices of the corresponding wage rates $\frac{r_i}{r_c}$:

$$\frac{p_i}{p_c} = \frac{r_i}{r_c}$$

And since wage rates move more or less proportionately in the two sections[1] marked cyclical fluctuations in $\frac{p_i}{p_c}$ are unlikely. This result is not impaired if we allow for changes in the technique of production. If the increase in productivity due to technical changes is different in consumption goods industries from that in investment goods industries this will, of course, influence the movement of $\frac{p_i}{p_c}$; but this influence can operate only in the long run, and is not of a *cyclical* nature. In order to investigate the movement of $\frac{p_i}{p_c}$ statistically we have constructed indices of the prices of finished consumption and investment goods in the U.S.A. for the period 1919–35. The index of consumption goods prices is a

[1] Wage rates in investment goods industries might be expected to fluctuate more, due to stronger changes in employment. In fact such is not the case, because trade unions are strongest in the heavy industry.

weighted average of the indices of the cost of living and the prices of motor cars,[1] that of investment goods— a weighted average of the building costs and the prices of movable equipment.[2]

The results are computed in the following table:

TABLE 3

Prices of Consumption and Investment Goods in U.S.A.
1929 = 100

	p_c	p_i	$\dfrac{p_i}{p_c}$		p_c	p_i	$\dfrac{p_i}{p_c}$
1919	102	110	108	1928	100	97	97
1920	119	125	105	1929	100	100	100
1921	105	105	100	1930	96	97	101
1922	98	94	96	1931	87	94	108
1923	101	101	100	1932	78	82	105
1924	101	101	100	1933	76	78	103
1925	104	98	94	1934	80	85	106
1926	103	98	95	1935	83	86	104
1927	101	96	95				

We see that variations in $\dfrac{p_i}{p_c}$ are in general small.

[1] The index of prices of motor cars is obtained from Dr. Kuznets' *National Income and Capital Formation, 1919–35*, by dividing the value of consumers' durable commodities in current prices by their value in 1929 prices (p. 40). The indices of cost of living and prices of motor cars are weighted in the proportion 88 : 12 according to the "composition of consumers' outlay" in 1929 (ibid., p. 59).

[2] The price index of movable equipment is obtained by dividing the value of "producers' durable commodities" at current prices by their value at 1929 prices (ibid., p. 40). The indices of building costs and of prices of movable equipment are weighted in proportion of 2 : 1 according to the amounts spent on these two types of investment (inclusive of maintenance) in 1929 (ibid., pp. 40 and 80).

At any rate, contrary to prevailing views there was no tendency for $\frac{p_i}{p_c}$ to fall in the depression 1930–33.

It is usually supposed that the prices of investment goods fluctuate much more violently than those of consumption goods. This is due to the assumption that increasing marginal-cost curves prevail in the short period; for if such were the case the larger proportionate fluctuations in the output of investment goods as compared with those in the output of consumption goods would lead to correspondingly larger fluctuations in the prices of investment goods. The statistical evidence of approximately proportional changes in the prices of the two types of goods indicates that the assumption of rising marginal-cost curves in the short period is unrealistic, and indirectly supports our assumption about the shape of short-period marginal-cost curves.

The important consequence of the above is that since $\frac{p_i}{p_c}$ has no marked cyclical fluctuations, changes in the ratio of the prices of investment and consumption goods may be neglected in the theory of the trade cycle. We make use of this conclusion in the last essay.

FINAL REMARKS

The results arrived at in this essay have a more general aspect. A world in which the degree of monopoly determines the distribution of the national income is a world far removed from the pattern of free competition.

Monopoly appears to be deeply rooted in the nature of the capitalist system: free competition, as an assumption, may be useful in the first stage of certain investigations, but as a description of the normal state of capitalist economy it is merely a myth.

2

INVESTMENT AND INCOME

1. The object of this essay is to clear up some questions arising out of the Keynesian theory of the Multiplier. We shall first deal with the equation between the expenditure on investment I and the value of savings S which has been so much discussed since *The General Theory* appeared. However, before embarking upon further argument we want to examine in detail one point often touched upon in this discussion: whether or not $I = S$ is a tautology. We define (as in the first essay, p. 14) the gross national income as the value added by all enterprises of an economy. Thus it is equal to total sales of all enterprises except those producing raw materials; i.e. to sales of goods to ultimate consumers + sales of newly produced fixed capital equipment + any increase in stocks and working capital. Sales of fixed capital equipment + increase in working capital and stocks may be called gross investment. Thus we have *by definition*:

National income = Sales of investment goods[1]

+ Sales of consumption goods

---

[1] Inclusive increase in working capital and stocks. This type of investment does not often involve a sale, the increase of inventories of a firm being created by its own production. Such case, however, may be considered as the firm's sale to itself.

where both national income and investment are gross concepts (from which maintenance and depreciation must be subtracted in order to obtain net national income and net investment respectively). Further, we shall call saving the difference between the national income as defined above and the expenditure on consumption. Thus we have, again *by definition*:

Sales of investment goods + Sales of consumption goods
= Saving + Expenditure by consumers

saving again being a gross concept. We have now the further equation:

Sales of consumption goods = Expenditure by consumers

which, however, is *not* a tautology since it represents the exchange process on the market of consumption goods (though it is an identity in the sense that it is fulfilled in all circumstances). Thus the equation derived from this exchange equation and the proceeding tautology:

Sales of investment goods = Saving

is also not a tautology. Now we take into account the exchange equation for the market of investment goods:

Sales of investment goods = Expenditure on investment

and we get finally:

Expenditure on investment = Saving

or:

$$I = S$$

It is useful to show how an increase in expenditure on investment by ΔI causes—by means of the exchange

43

process on the market of investment and consumption goods—saving S to increase by an amount ΔS equal to ΔI.

If in a certain period the expenditure on investment is I and in the next $I + \Delta I$, sales of investment goods must increase by ΔI. If the output of them was not changed, the total amount ΔI is an addition to income of capitalists (entrepreneurs and rentiers), but if output and employment also increase a part of ΔI is received by workers. Out of the addition to income ΔI flowing to the investment goods industries a part ΔS_1 is saved while another part $\Delta I - \Delta S_1$ is consumed. This last amount makes for an additional expenditure on consumption goods.

Consider now the consumption goods industries: a part of the total sales of consumption goods is bought by the capitalists and workers in consumption goods industries, the rest is purchased by the capitalists and workers in investment goods industries. And it is the value of this latter which is equal to the savings "in consumption goods industries" S , for it is equal to the difference between the total sales of consumption goods and the expenditure on consumption by the capitalists and workers drawing income from their production. Thus an additional expenditure on consumption by the capitalists and workers in the investment goods industries creates an equal additional saving ΔS_2. We have:

$$\Delta I - \Delta S_1 = \Delta S_2$$

or:

$$\Delta I = \Delta S_1 + \Delta S_2 = \Delta S$$

44

and we see how an additional expenditure on investment ΔI creates an equal addition to saving ΔS.

2. It may be interesting to notice that the above equations are contained in the famous Marxian scheme of "extended reproduction."[1] Marx even considers the questions of how to provide "means" for increased expenditure on investment.[2] It must be added, however, that the problems discussed here are treated by Marx from a rather special point of view. He is interested in finding out, with the help of exchange equations, the pace of investment in investment and consumption goods industries respectively, which is necessary in order to secure a steady expansion of output. (The rates of profit in both divisions of industry are assumed to be equal throughout and on this basis the process of expansion is constructed so as to make investment in each, at the end of every "production-exchange cycle," equal to its saving so that there is no "shift of capital" from consumption to investment goods industries or conversely.) He does not pay attention to the problem of what happens if investment is inadequate to secure the moving equilibrium, and therefore does not approach the idea of the key position of investment in the determination of the level of total output and employment.

Exactly the reverse attitude is represented by one of his eminent pupils, Rosa Luxemburg. In her *Akkumulation des Kapitals* she stressed the point that, if capitalists are saving, their profits can be "realized" only if a

[1] *Capital*, Vol. II, *The process of circulation of Capital*, London, Swan Sonnenschein & Co., pp. 571–611.　　[2] Ibid., p. 593.

corresponding amount is spent by them on investment. She, however, considered impossible the persistence of net investment (at least in the long run) in a closed capitalist economy; thus, according to her, it is only the existence of exports to the non-capitalist countries which allows for the expansion of a capitalist system. The theory cannot be accepted as a whole, but the necessity of covering the "gap of saving" by home investment or exports was outlined by her perhaps more clearly than anywhere else before the publication of Mr. Keynes's *General Theory*.

3. We tacitly assumed in the first paragraph that we were dealing with a closed economy. In an open economy the national income is equal to home sales of goods to consumers + home sales of (newly produced) fixed capital equipment + increase in working capital and stocks + foreign balance of goods and services. Following an argument analogous to that of the first paragraph we obtain the equation:

$$\left.\begin{array}{l}\text{Expenditure on investment}\\ \text{Balance of foreign countries'}\\ \qquad \text{expenditure}\end{array}\right\} = \text{Saving}$$

An increment in the balance of foreign countries' expenditure home investment remaining constant, creates in the same way as shown in the first paragraph an equal increament of savings. (This, I think, is the correct interpretation of the theory of Rosa Luxemburg.)

4. We simplified tacitly in another respect also our argument in paragraph one, namely, we abstracted the

46

complications arising out of Government income and expenditure. The value added by private enterprise does not coincide with the total income of capitalists and labour, for a part is transferred by taxation to the Government.[1] We do *not* consider, as is often done, this part as the equivalent of consumption of Governmental services. (We mean here by consumption only the voluntary spending for goods and services.) The Government in turn spends its revenue partly on officials' salaries, doles for unemployed, etc., and interest on the public debt; while the rest of the revenue, being devoted to Governmental investment[2] and to the increase in Governmental claims, constitutes Governmental saving.

Thus the consumption of people drawing their income from the Government is included in consumption; a part of saving is done by the Government; and a part of the output of investment goods is sold to the Government. The national income can therefore be represented in the following two ways:

Private investment[3]	Private saving
Governmental investment	Governmental saving
Balance of foreign countries expenditure	Consumption
Consumption	

Let us subtract from both sides Governmental saving. As Governmental investment less Governmental saving

[1] By Government are meant here all public authorities.
[2] Armaments, public buildings, etc.
[3] Inclusive residential building.

constitutes the budget deficit or the "balance of Government's expenditure" we obtain:

Private expenditure on investment	Private saving
Balance of Governments' expenditure	Consumption
Balance of foreign countries' expenditure	
Consumption	

The sum of private saving plus (voluntary) consumption may be called private national income Y. It is equal to the value added by all enterprises less Governmental saving and also to the sum of all private incomes after the deduction of taxes.[1] It is this definition of "national income" which we shall mean in the following argument. The sum: private home investment + balance of foreign countries expenditure + balance of Governmental expenditure will be denoted by I, and private saving by S. Thus the equation:

$$I = S$$

refers now to investment in the above sense and to private saving.

It may be useful to show how the increase in the balance of Governmental expenditure (the other two components of I remaining constant) creates an equal increase in private saving. Let us suppose, e.g., that

[1] Both direct and indirect. Thus the value of consumption is here reckoned at prices from which excise, etc., have been deducted.

the Government increases officials' salaries by ΔI by borrowing to that extent. The officials save out of their additional revenue ΔS_1 and spend $\Delta I - \Delta S_1$. Thus the sales of consumption goods industries to people other than capitalists and workers attached to these industries increases by the amount of officials' additional expenditure $\Delta I - \Delta S_1$. But the sales of consumption goods industries to "outsiders" is equal to the saving of capitalists and workers attached to these industries. Consequently savings "in consumption goods industries" rise by $\Delta I - \Delta S_1$. Since the savings of officials increase by ΔS_1 total private saving rises by $\Delta I - \Delta S_1 + \Delta S_1 = \Delta I$, i.e. by the increment in the balance of Government's expenditure.

It is interesting to notice that here the rise of "investment" by ΔI (creating an equal increase in private saving) causes *directly* a rise of consumption by $\Delta I - \Delta S_1$. If the Government spends the amount borrowed ΔI for additional dole payment, ΔS_1 may be supposed equal to zero because dole receivers do not save. Then the rise of "investment" by ΔI *directly* increases consumption also by ΔI.

5. Changes in the three components of I: private investment, the balance of Governmental expenditure and the balance of foreign countries' expenditure are in general interconnected. The most typical interconnection is the influence of a "primary" change in private investment on the other two components. An increment in home private investment, by raising employment and income, reduces dole payments and increases the tax

revenue so that the deficit tends to fall. An increase in output and consumption also requires more foreign raw materials, foodstuffs, etc., which tends to diminish the balance of trade. Thus the stimulating influence of an increase in private home investment on employment and income is hampered by a decrease in the other two components of I.

SPECIAL ASSUMPTIONS

1. In our further argument we shall use some results reached in the first essay. We saw there that the relative share of manual labour in the national income shows great stability in a moderately long period. In the first essay we defined national income as the value added by all enterprises of an economy; now, however, we mean by it "private national income" which is less than the value added by all enterprises by the amount of Governmental saving. But since the latter bears a small proportion to the national income, the ratio of the wage bill to the "private national income" Y is not appreciably changed.

The wage bill is the income of employed manual workers before the deduction of taxes. Their spendable income is thus less than the wage bill, but if changes in the system of taxation do not occur we can assume it approximately proportionate to the wage bill. From that we can conclude that the ratio of manual workers' spendable income to Y, which we denote by a, must also show great stability. The rest of the national income represents the income of all non-wage earners after the deduction of taxes. We denote it by y; it includes the incomes of capitalists, salary earners, and also dole receivers. We have then:

$$y = (1 - a) Y^1 \quad . \quad . \quad . \quad . \quad . \quad (6)$$

The savings of manual workers are so small that we can neglect them[2] and thus identify total private saving S with non-wage earners' savings. Hence we can now write the investment-saving equation in the form:

$$I = S = s$$

But s is, of course, equal to the difference between income y and consumption c of non-wage earners.

$$I = y - c \quad . \quad . \quad . \quad . \quad . \quad (7)$$

It is clear that the equation (6) and (7) establish a functional relation between investment I and national income Y if such a relation exists between non-wage earners' income y and the consumption out of it c. Here, however, we touch upon the problem how to measure the amounts dealt with. For we clearly cannot expect a definite functional relation between income and the consumption out of it unless both are expressed in "real" terms.

2. We shall express investment, income, and consump-

---

[1] Since a is equal to about $0 \cdot 38$ in Great Britain and about $0 \cdot 32$ in U.S.A. (with shop assistants classified as manual labour) the stability of $1 - a$ is much greater than that of a.

[2] a is in general smaller than $1 - a$, while the proportion of savings in workers' income is incomparably lower than that in y.

tion in "stable values" by deflating them with the index of prices of finished (consumption and investment) goods. This index has for this purpose the following advantage. It was established in the preceding essay (pp. 38–39) that the index of prices of finished consumption goods (cost of living) and the index prices of finished investment goods (building costs and prices of movable equipment) tend to deviate only slightly from each other. Thus if we deflate income and consumption with the joint index of prices of finished goods (composed of these two indices) we get figures approximately equal to "real" income and consumption, i.e. to income and consumption deflated with the index of finished consumption goods. And similarly investment (which is largely in *fixed* capital) is deflated with an index not much different from that of prices of finished investment goods.

We do not use here the Keynesian wage-units because even in not very long periods there is a considerable change in the productivity of labour due to technical progress. Thus income measured in wage-units often fails to be an adequate indicator of the "real" income.

INVESTMENT AND INCOME IN A SIMPLIFIED MODEL

1. We noticed above that the equations:

$$y = (1 - a)Y \quad . \quad . \quad . \quad . \quad . \quad (6)$$

and

$$I = y - c \quad . \quad . \quad . \quad . \quad . \quad (7)$$

enable us to establish a functional relation between national income Y and investment I provided we can

52

establish such a relation between the income of non-wage earners y and their consumption c. Before inquiring into the connection between y and c in the real world we shall apply the above equations to the analysis of investment and income in a simplified model.

We assume that in this hypothetical economy the joint consumption of capitalists, salary earners and dole receivers c expressed in "stable values" is constant. We denote this constant by c_0 and thus we obtain from equations (1) and (2):

$$Y = \frac{1}{1-a}I + \frac{c_0}{1-a}$$

It is easy to see that the ratio of an increment of income ΔY to the corresponding increments of investment ΔI is equal to $\frac{1}{1-a}$:

$$\frac{\Delta Y}{\Delta I} = \frac{1}{1-a}$$

Thus $\frac{1}{1-a}$ is the multiplier which has in our system a constant value. It does not follow, of course, that the ratio of income to investment $\frac{Y}{I}$ is also constant. On the contrary, it follows from the above equation that $\frac{Y}{I}$ falls with the increase of investment. This means that investment must fluctuate more than national income and *a fortiori* more than consumption (for national income is the sum of consumption and investment).

The formula of the multiplier shows that if some

53

increase in the rate of investment has occurred income must have increased by an amount which is $\dfrac{1}{1-a}$ times as great. Therefore, the multiplier cannot tell us what would happen if, e.g., public works financed by State borrowing were undertaken since other kinds of investment might increase or fall off in consequence. If, however, we can demonstrate that in the period considered this influence is negligible, then the multiplier will show approximately what will be the increase in income.

Our discussion of the investment-saving equation in the first section demonstrates that there is no "magic" in the working of the multiplier. Suppose we know that in a certain year the total expenditure on investment was greater by ΔI than in the preceding year, then savings must have increased by the same amount. But since the manual workers do not save and since in our model the consumption of other classes is constant, this means that the incomes of the latter increased by the amount ΔI. As, however, the ratio of the distribution of income between manual workers and all other classes is steadily $\dfrac{a}{1-a}$ output must have expanded so that the rise of non-wage earners' incomes by ΔI was accompanied by a rise of $\dfrac{1}{1-a} \cdot \Delta I$ in the wage bill, the total increase in income being:

$$\Delta I + \Delta I \cdot \frac{a}{1-a} = \frac{\Delta I}{1-a}$$

2. There is a point in the "working of the multiplier" which, I think, requires special explanation. If an increase in the expenditure on investment, e.g. in fixed capital, takes place, an additional demand for consumption goods arises. But how can the production of them, which even with given capital equipment requires a certain time, immediately rise? Such a rise is not at all impossible, because existing stocks of raw materials and semi-manufactures may be immediately converted into working capital and enable the factories to supply the market without delay with finished consumption goods. If, however, for this or any other reason such a process of adjustment does not occur with sufficient speed, stocks of finished consumption goods are depleted and in the formula of the multiplier ΔI is equal to the difference between the additional investment in fixed capital and any consequential dis-investment in stocks in the period considered.

What happens, however, if no reserves of raw materials, semi-manufactures, and finished consumption goods are in existence, and thus the supply of consumption goods is fully inelastic at the time? The multiplier is then equal to *1*, since the volume of consumption does not increase and our formula appears wrong. This is due to the fact that our assumption of the constancy of the relative share of manual labour a in the national income is incompatible with an inelastic supply of consumption goods. For in this case the increase of employment in investment good industries must cause a shift in the national income to the disadvantage of the workers.

Since according to statistical evidence a tends to be stable we can exclude from our consideration the case of an inelastic supply of consumption goods.

INCOME AND CONSUMPTION IN THE REAL WORLD

1. We pass now from our simplified model to real conditions. The consumption of non-wage earners is no longer supposed to be stable. It is clear that there must be *some* connection between their income y and the consumption c out of it. (Both are supposed to be expressed in "stable values.") Various objections, however, may be raised against this connection being close.

The first is that consumption out of a given income or "the propensity to consume" is greatly affected by the level of the rate of interest. In classical economics the stimulating influence of a rise in the rate of interest upon the thrift was strongly emphasized. It has, however, long been indicated that it is not at all certain whether consumption is really encouraged or discouraged by a higher rate of interest. But all this discussion appears to be of a rather academic character, at least as concerns development in the moderately long period with which we are here concerned. For in such periods the long-term rate shows but small changes (see pp. 112–113), and clearly this is the rate which is relevant here. Thus we can safely neglect the influence of the rate of interest in the analysis of the connection between y and c.

2. Another very important objection is that capitalists' expenditure is only loosely connected with their income because their "propensity to consume" depends to great

56

extent on the actual level of capital values; in particular on that of stock exchange prices. For if he feels wealthier, the capitalist may assume less thrifty habits, even though his current real income has not altered.

Or one can imagine him being influenced not by the *level* of actual capital valuations but by the *change* in these valuations within the period considered. For he may be supposed to consider as income not only his current revenue but also the windfall gain or loss due to changes in the valuation of his assets.

It is idle to discuss theoretically the problem of whether these factors are more or less important in the determination of capitalist consumption. And since the period of American stock exchange boom 1926–29 is often considered typical in this respect, it will be useful to look at the revelant figures in these years.

In the table on p. 58 are given the gross and net income of capitalists,[1] the approximate value of capitalists' consumption,[2] the index of stock exchange prices, and

---

[1] Based on Dr. Kuznets' *National Income and Capital Formation, 1919–1935*, p. 24. Income tax not deducted.

[2] This is calculated in the following way. We deduct from the income of capitalists the total investment (also Kuznets' estimate) and thus obtain the capitalists' consumption less the saving of workers (chiefly of salary earners because that of manual workers is small). Further, from *America's Capacity to Consume* we estimate the average rate of saving of all workers (black coat and manual) in 1929 as 6 per cent. Since the size and distribution of workers' income did not change very much in the period 1920–29, we applied the same rate to all years and thus obtained approximate figures for workers' saving, which we added to the figures of capitalists' consumption less the saving of workers.

57

the change of this index from the beginning to the end of each year. It must be added that in the period 1926–29 commodity prices were stable and thus there is no necessity to deflate the money values.

	($ *milliards*)			
	1926	1927	1928	1929
Gross capitalists' income (before deduction for depreciation and maintenance)	41·9	39·3	42·1	42·9
Net capitalists' income (after deduction for depreciation and maintenance)	26·5	24·1	25·7	25·9
Approximate capitalists' consumption	21·7	19·0	22·4	20·7
Prices of shares (Standard Statistics, 1926 = 100, yearly averages) ..	100·0	118·3	149·9	190·0
Change in the prices of shares (the change of the same index from the beginning to the end of a given year)	+ 3·8	+ 31·6	+ 40·1	− 33·7

Both capitalists' income and capitalists' consumption show small changes in the same direction. Share prices are violently rising throughout the period and the change of share prices from the beginning to the end of the year (measuring the windfall loss or gain) varies greatly in different years. (In 1928 *both* figures are much greater than in the preceding years.) The only possible interpretation of these data is that the influence of the stock exchange on capitalists' consumption in U.S.A. in 1926–29 was not very great. But if the stock exchange did not greatly influence the capitalists' propensity to consume even under such favourable circumstances its influence cannot generally be very important.

3. Another argument is directed against the existence not so much of a functional relation between the consumption and income of capitalists but rather of one between their current consumption and their current income. It is not here denied that an appreciable time-lag exists between y and the corresponding c (as opposed to income and consumption of manual workers). This modifies but does not invalidate the "theory of the multiplier." We are introducing this modification at the final stage of our argument (see pp. 66–68).

4. A further argument against a close connection between c and y refers to the variations in the distribution of income. The earners of y fall into various groups with "different propensities to consume" and, consequently, it is not only the change in the amount of y but also the shifts in its distribution which determine the fluctuations of c.

We can distinguish the following groups among non-wage earners: (1) dole receivers (unemployed, etc.); (2) salaried employees; (3) small entrepreneurs; (4) rentiers; (5) dividend receivers; (6) joint stock companies (the gross income of the last consists of depreciation and net corporative savings).

Considerable shifts in the distribution of income among these groups occur in the trade cycle and obviously affect their joint consumption c, but it can be shown that these shifts are strongly correlated with changes in the volume of y (expressed in stable values) and thus c is a fairly close function of y.

It is easy to see that the distribution of non-wage earners' income y among the various groups is *grosso modo* determined by: (1) the volume of y itself; (2) the index of prices of finished goods, p, with which we deflated the incomes; (3) the dole rate; (4) the average salary rate. Indeed y and p determine the money value of non-wage earners' incomes yp. Further, y bears a constant proportion to national income Y and the latter varies inversely with the amount of unemployment. Thus given y and the dole rate, the aggregate dole payment is determined. In a similar way y and the average salary rate determine the salary bill. Subtracting dole payments and the salary bill from yp, we obtain the money value of capitalists' incomes. Now the aggregate interest on loan debt is approximately stable (in money terms) over the moderately long period and can be considered as given. Subtracting it from total capitalist income, we obtain dividends and entrepreneurial incomes. It may now be easily shown that the changes in the distribution of non-wage earners' income y depend to great extent on those in its volume. For a fall, say, in y (which is proportionate to the national income Y) means, of course, a decline in output and employment, and this depresses in a more or less definite way the salary rate and the prices of finished goods (which, according to results arrived at in the preceding

60

essay, p. 37, move more or less proportionately to the wage cost). Thus the chief factors determining the distribution of non-wage earners' income can be reduced to function of its volume y.[1]

The effect of the fall in y will be to increase the relative share of dole receivers, salary earners, and rentiers. This is clear as regards dole receivers and rentiers. As concerns salary earners, the proportionate fall in the salary bill in the slump is always smaller than that in the wage bill; while, as the relative share of manual labour in the national income is constant, the total income of non-wage earners must change proportionately to the wage bill. Thus the proportion that the salary bill bears to the total non-wage earners' income must rise when y falls.

To the rise in the relative share of dole receivers, salary earners, and rentiers in y as y diminishes, corresponds the sharp fall in the relative share in y going to corporations (in the form of depreciation and net corporative savings). The change in the income of small entrepreneurs and in dividends follows a middle course and is likely neither to rise nor to fall very much relatively to the total income of non-wage earners.

It therefore follows that the shift in the distribution of non-wage earners' income y when it is declining tends to hamper the fall of consumption c out of it, i.e. c falls less than it would if the distribution of y did not alter. If y rises c increases less than it would if there were no shifts in the distribution of y.

[1] Except the dole rate, which thus must be treated as datum.

INVESTMENT AND INCOME IN THE REAL WORLD

1. As a result of the above investigation it can be said that on certain assumptions—which are usually fulfilled in the moderately long period—and neglecting provisionally the time lag between income and consumption, a more or less close connection between c and y is likely to exist. Thus we can write:

$$c = \eta(y) \qquad . \quad . \quad . \quad . \quad . \ (8)$$

As already mentioned above (p. 51), this equation enables us to establish the functional relation between investment I and national income Y. For besides the equation (8) we have the equation

$$I = y - c \qquad . \quad . \quad . \quad . \quad . \ (7)$$

which expresses the fact that investment, since it is equal to total saving, is also equal to that of non-wage earners alone, because the saving of wage earners is negligible. Further, the relative share of manual labour in the national income is a constant a and thus we have for non-wage earners income y:

$$y = (1 - a)Y \quad . \quad . \quad . \quad . \ (6)$$

From the equations (7) and (8) it follows that I is a function of y, which in conjunction with equation (6) shows that there must be a functional relationship between investment I and the national income Y.

Consequently we can write

$$Y = f(I) \qquad . \quad . \quad . \quad . \quad . \ (9)$$

where f is, of course, an increasing function, and from this equation we obtain the multiplier:

$$\frac{\Delta Y}{\Delta I} = f'(I)$$

It is interesting to see how the multiplier works in the real world. If we have an increase in investment from level I to a given level $I + \Delta I$, there is an increase in employment, output, and national income. If, as in our simplified model, the consumption of non-wage earners c remained stationary, this increase would be pushed to the point at which non-wage earners' income increases by ΔI; for at that point non-wage earners save ΔI more, and by assumption they would not tend to expand their consumption. But in reality when their income increases they do consume more. And thus the rise of employment output and income stops only when that level of non-wage earners' income is reached at which their increased saving and consumption are such as to correspond to their propensity to consume. Consequently the multiplier is in the real world greater than in our simplified model. And since in the latter it was equal $\frac{1}{1-a}$ (where a is the relative share of manual labour in the national income) we have:

$$\frac{\Delta Y}{\Delta I} = f'(I) > \frac{1}{1-a}$$

How much $f'(I)$ exceeds $\frac{1}{1-a}$ depends on the thrift habits of the various groups of non-wage earners and on the redistribution of income between these groups associated with the rise of their total income y.

2. The consumption of non-wage earners, c, changes always in a lesser proportion than their income y, and for two reasons. First, each individual's consumption is less elastic than his saving; and, second, the redistribution of y associated with the change in its amount, is—as shown above—such as to reduce the resultant change in c (since a rise of y is accompanied by an increase in the relative share of it going to corporations and conversely).

Since the consumption of non-wage earners changes in a lesser proportion than their income the reverse must be true of their saving, i.e. the latter must change always in a greater proportion than y. From this results an important feature of the function connecting national income Y with investment I. Since I is equal to the saving of non-wage earners it must change always in a greater proportion than their income y. But the latter bears a constant proportion to the national income Y. Thus investment rises or falls always in a greater proportion than the national income. The shape of the function f is such that $\dfrac{I}{f(I)}$ increases when I rises. In other words, investment fluctuates more violently than national income and *a fortiori* more violently than consumption.

3. The last proposition has been known in economics for a long time, but it was deduced from the so-called acceleration principle. The argument ran thus: Let us assume that at a certain time the volume of capital

equipment is 20, the output of consumption goods 10, and gross investment 1·5, of which depreciation is 1 and new investment 0·5. If now consumption increases in a period by 10 per cent to 11, equipment must increase in the same proportion to 22. Thus net investment in this period must be 2. (There will also be some increase in depreciation because of the increase in the amount of capital equipment, but it will be negligible.) Thus while consumption increases by only 10 per cent, gross investment rises from 1 + 0·5 to 1 + 2, i.e. by 100 per cent.

The argument is apparently based on the unrealistic assumption that the degree of use of equipment is constant; while it is clear from trade cycle statistics that it is precisely the fluctuation in the use of equipment which accounts chiefly for changes in output, and the proportionate increase or decrease of equipment is of minor importance. Consequently the connection between investment and consumption given by the acceleration principle is also unrealistic: for according to this principle investment is an increasing function of the rate of *change* in consumption. Thus on the top of the boom when consumption is stationary investment should fall to the level of depreciation, while the statistics show that its maximum is reached almost simultaneously with that of consumption. (See, e.g., statistical data in the next section.)

This is, however, in accordance with the connection between investment and consumption which was established above on a quite different basis. Starting from the equation of saving and investment and making some assumptions about the distribution of the national

65   E

income among various classes and about their propensity to consume, we demonstrated that national income and, therefore, consumption is an increasing function of investment, which, however, changes always in a greater proportion than consumption.[1]

4. We have now to make the modification which we promised in connection with the existence of the time-lag between non-wage earners' income y and consumption

[1] A new interpretation of the acceleration principle was given by R. F. Harrod in *The Trade Cycle*. The material modification introduced by him is that it is not the actual investment but investment decisions or orders which are a function of the rate of change in consumption. In this form the acceleration principle *is* compatible with the theory of the multiplier. For there is a time-lag between investment orders and actual investment, and thus they are in general not equal; consequently it is possible that the rate of investment decisions is an increasing function of the *change in consumption*, while *consumption itself* is a function of the rate of actual investment.

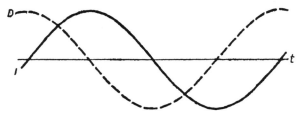

But this theory is also unrealistic. It implies that the rate of investment decisions D is an increasing function of the change in the rate of actual investment I, and therefore that the respective time curves are situated as shown on the chart. It is easy to see that the period is then four times the time-lag between D and I. Since the average time-lag between investment decisions and investment output is unlikely to be greater than half a year (see p. 127), the period of trade cycle would be less than 2 years; while its actual length is 7–12 years.

out of it c. This time-lag results in the present national income being influenced not only by the present but also by past investment. Consequently the system behaves as if a certain delay were involved in the functional connection between investment and income. Thus if we denote investment and income at time t by I_t and Y_t respectively our equation (9) must be written:

$$Y_t = f(I_{t-\lambda}) \quad . \quad . \quad . \quad . \quad . \quad (10)$$

where λ is the time-lag between investment and income.[1]

The multiplier may be defined as:

$$\frac{\Delta Y_t}{\Delta I_{t-\lambda}} = f'(I_{t-\lambda})$$

[1] Let us denote the time-lag between y and c by ω. Then we have:

$$c_t = \eta(y_{t-\omega})$$

and the equation between investment and non-wage earners' saving gives:

$$I_t = y_t - \eta(y_{t-\omega})$$

On the other hand, it is clear from p. 62 that the formula (10) can be established if the time-lag fulfils the equation:

$$I_t = y_{t+\lambda} - \eta(y_{t+\lambda})$$

Thus λ must fulfil the equation:

$$y_t - \eta(y_{t-\omega}) = y_{t+\lambda} - \eta(y_{t+\lambda})$$

or: $\qquad y_{t+\lambda} - y_t = \eta(y_{t+\lambda}) - \eta(y_{t-\omega})$

We divide this equation by $y_{t+\lambda} - y_{t-\omega}$:

$$\frac{y_{t+\lambda} - y_t}{y_{t+\lambda} - y_{t-\omega}} = \frac{\eta(y_{t+\lambda}) - \eta(y_{t-\omega})}{y_{t+\lambda} - y_{t-\omega}}$$

If the time-lags are small and the time-curve y_t continuous, we obtain as a good approximation:

$$\frac{\lambda}{\lambda + \omega} = \eta'(y_t)$$

which defines λ in terms of ω and η'. If ω and η' are slowly changing variables, as they are likely to be, the same is true of λ.

The time-lag λ being in general not constant, and the function not quite stable, what is the real meaning of equation (10)? It may be formulated in the following way: there exists such a function f and such a constant λ that the deviations of Y_t from $f(I_{t-\lambda})$ are relatively small.

A STATISTICAL ILLUSTRATION

1. We are using, as a statistical illustration of the above, data on national income and investment in the U.S.A. computed in Dr. Kuznets' *National Income and Capital Formation, 1919–35.*

In order to obtain the "gross private national income" Y we subtract from gross income (including repairs of equipment) of all private industries the Government's[1] gross saving (pp. 14, 80, 18).

The latter subtracted from gross capital formation (inclusive of repairs, pp. 40, 80) gives investment I in our sense of the term. The results are represented in the following table :

TABLE 4

Gross National Income and Investment in the U.S.A.

($ *milliards*)

	Y	I		Y	I
1919	79·3	31·3	1928	86·0	22·9
1920	82·4	29·1	1929	89·7	25·5
1921	65·3	17·1	1930	79·6	19·4
1922	64·6	17·7	1931	63·0	13·6
1923	74·8	22·4	1932	44·6	7·0
1924	74·7	18·9	1933	42·1	7·4
1925	78·7	22·7	1934	51·8	10·6
1926	84·3	23·2	1935	58·7	14·9
1927	81·8	22·3			

[1] We mean by Government as above all public authorities.

In order to obtain "stable values" we must deflate these items with the index of prices of finished goods given in the next table. This was constructed from the indices of prices of finished consumption and investment goods in the U.S.A. computed on p. 39.[1]

TABLE 5

Index of Prices of Finished Goods in the U.S.A

1929 = 100

1919	104	1925	102	1931	89
1920	120	1926	102	1932	78
1921	105	1927	100	1933	76
1922	97	1928	99	1934	81
1923	101	1929	100	1935	84
1924	101	1930	96		

Deflating with this index the money values of national income and investmens contained in Table 2, we obtain:

TABLE 6

Gross National Income and Investment in the U.S.A.
(*In $ milliards at 1929 prices*)

	Y	I		Y	I
1919	76·1	30·0	1928	86·9	23·1
1920	68·7	24·2	1929	89·7	25·5
1921	62·3	16·3	1930	82·8	20·2
1922	66·6	18·2	1931	70·8	15·3
1923	74·0	22·2	1932	56·5	8·9
1924	74·0	18·7	1933	54·4	9·7
1925	77·1	22·3	1934	64·0	13·1
1926	82·6	22·5	1935	70·0	17·8
1927	81·8	22·3			

[1] We have weighted them in the proportion 3 : 1 according to the composition of the gross national product inclusive of repairs in 1929. *National Income and Capital Formation*, pp. 45, 80.

2. Plotting the figures on a diagram (see Fig. 3), we see at a glance that while the points corresponding to the period 1924–35 are scattered round the straight line AB, those corresponding to 1919–23 lie far above it. The points 1919 and 1920 are the highest, and below them are the points 1921, 1922, and 1923 round the straight line A_1B_1 parallel to AB.

This can be interpreted as a shift of the investment-income curve. There was evidently a sharp increase in the propensity to consume in the period 1919–24. A shifting of the investment-income curve in the long run is of course a quite normal phenomenon. Here, however, we have a change of a rather discontinuous character. We do not here attempt to account for this shift, which presents a problem requiring special investigation, but will only examine in more detail the period 1924–35, during which we notice a more or less stable connection between investment and income.

The way in which the points 1924–35 are scattered round AB shows a certain regularity: looking at them in the chronological order (treating both 1926–27 and 1928–29 as biennia, which are denoted on the chart by white circles), they form a polygon rotating in a clockwise direction. This shows that there is a time-lag between investment and income. Indeed, the straight line AB represents in such circumstances the approximate connection between investment in a year considered and income at a later date. For instance, to investment in 1931 corresponds the abscissa of the point M lying between 1931 and 1932. On the

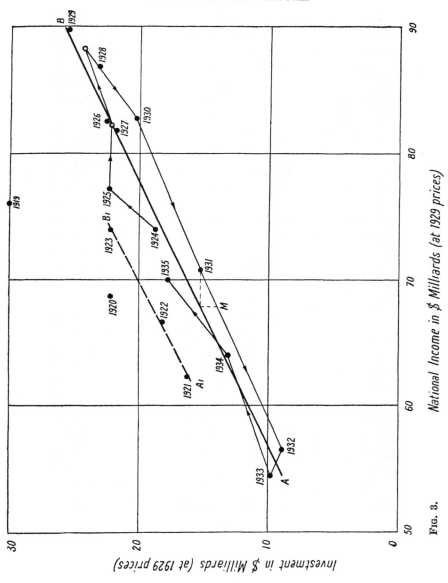

FIG. 3.

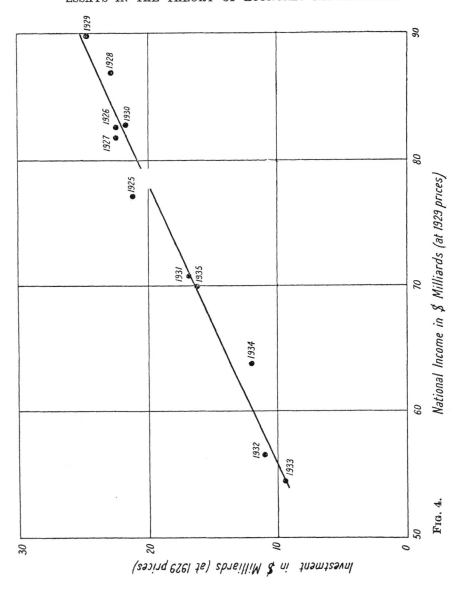

FIG. 4.

basis of our polygon it is possible to determine the average time-lag. It appears that it is here equal to about four months.

Thus we see that a correlation between present income and investment $0 \cdot 33$ years ago must obtain. (For instance, the income in 1931 corresponds to investment four months earlier which we determine by adding $\frac{2}{3}$ of investment in 1931 to $\frac{1}{3}$ of investment in 1930.) The results are again plotted on a diagram (Fig. 4). The ordinates of the points plotted now represent not I_t but $I_{t-0\cdot33}$. The deviations from the line of best fit are now relatively small. The equation of this line is:

$$Y_t = 2\cdot25\, I_{t-0\cdot33} + 33\cdot2 \qquad (11)$$

It represents the function f for U.S.A. in the period 1924–35. It proves, as is easy to see, the rule (p. 64) that income changes in a lesser proportion than investment. (It is obvious that the ratio $\dfrac{Y_t}{I_{t-0\cdot33}}$ falls when investment increases.) The multiplier $\dfrac{\Delta Y_t}{\Delta I_{t-0\cdot33}}$ is equal to $2\cdot25$. As shown on p. 63 the multiplier must be greater than $\dfrac{1}{1-a}$ where a is the relative share of manual labour in the national income. According to my rough estimate a for U.S.A. is about $0\cdot32$, and thus $\dfrac{1}{1-a}$ is about $1\cdot5$. Thus this rule also is proved.

The line of best fit is here a straight one. But prob-

73

ably this is not the case outside the range of income and investment here considered.

Fig. 5 compares the actual national income and that calculated from formula (11).

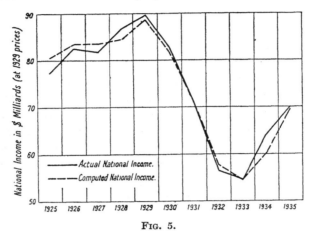

FIG. 5.

74

MONEY AND REAL WAGES

INTRODUCTION

We intend in this essay to discuss at some length the Keynesian theory of wages. We are limiting ourselves to the consideration of a closed economy, for this is the only case to which the Keynesian argument fully applies. To take an extreme example, let us imagine an economy which exports all its produce and imports all consumption goods. It is obvious that in such an economy a reduction in money wages is equivalent to one in real wages, and increases output and employment (but not necessarily the real wage bill).

A SIMPLIFIED MODEL

1. In order not to confuse the various questions involved we shall first consider the problem of wages in a highly simplified model. We assume for the moment: (1) that free competition prevails; (2) that the salary earners and manual workers do not save; (3) that the various types of wages and salaries change always in the same proportion; (4) that entrepreneurs and rentiers have an equal propensity to consume; (5) that the rate of interest is kept constant. All these simplifying assumptions will be gradually removed afterwards.

2. Since in our model free competition prevails, the

short-period equilibrium of a firm is reached at the point of intersection of the horizontal "individual" demand curve and the upward sloping part of the short-period marginal-cost curve. Thus with an increase in employment the ratio of prices to wages must increase, or, what amounts to the same, the real wages must fall (if there is no rise in the productivity of labour due to changes in technique or intensity of work). This is the "classical" doctrine of real wages, and is admitted also by Keynes. As we shall see below, this rule does not apply to real conditions of imperfect competition as described in the essay on "The Distribution of the National Income," but it holds good in the model now considered.

3. We will now deal with the problem of changes in money wages in our system. But before going into the matter some general remarks are necessary.

The national income may be represented in two ways as follows:

| Capitalists' income | Investment |
| Wages and salaries | Consumption |

Since in our model the consumption of salary earners and manual workers is equal to their income, we obtain by subtracting wages and salaries from both sides:

Capitalists' income = Investment

+ Capitalists' consumption

This equation is very important for the further argument. It follows from it that capitalists' income

76

expressed in "stable values" is fully determined by the volume of investment and capitalists' consumption.

It will perhaps be useful to look at this simple but paradoxical theorem in a different way.[1] Let us schematically represent our economy as consisting of three industries, producing wage-goods, investment goods, and goods consumed by capitalists (or luxury goods) respectively. Wage-goods are in part consumed by the workers producing them, while the surplus sold to workers of the other two industries constitutes capitalists' income derived from the wage-goods industry. Thus employment in the investment and luxury goods industries determines capitalists' income in the wage-goods industry expressed in "stable values." But capitalists' incomes drawn from investment and luxury goods production (expressed in "stable values") are of course also determined by employment in these two industries. Thus the output of investment and luxury goods determines total capitalists' income expressed in "stable values." And because capitalists' income from the wage-goods industry is equal to workers' income in the other two industries the value of capitalists' total income is equal to the value of the output of investment and luxury goods.

4. Let us now consider what happens when all wages and salaries are reduced in the same proportion. If the

[1] The above equation is of course equivalent (under the assumption that the salary earners and manual workers do not save) to the equality of saving and investment which can be obtained from it by subtracting the capitalists' consumption from both sides.

capitalists, having succeeded in cutting wages, immediately raise the volume of their consumption and investment in the expectation of higher profits, employment must increase. Indeed, capitalists' income expressed in "stable values" must rise by the same amount that the volume of their consumption and investment has risen, and this can be attained only by an increase in employment. And the latter is connected in our model with the fall of real wages, which therefore decline as a result of a decline in money wages.

Or to represent this process in a different way: employment in the luxury goods and investment goods industries increases because of the rise in effective demand on the part of capitalists and employment in the wage-goods industry rises because of the demand on the part of workers set to work in the other two industries. This rise in employment, as shown in the preceding paragraph, is just sufficient to raise profits by the same amount that capitalists' consumption and investment have risen.

Such a state of affairs is, however, extremely unlikely. First, entrepreneurs will in general not hurry with new investment orders simply on the strength of a successful wage reduction, but will rather wait until the expectations of higher profitability have been realized. Even should they give new orders at once, the technical time-lag between investment orders and the actual production of investment goods would prevent the latter from increasing immediately.

The position as regards capitalists' consumption is similar, in that it is actual rather than expected income which influences the capitalists' standard of living, and, as was shown in the preceding essay, even this influence operates with considerable delay.

If the above is a true description of the course of events, then a wage cut cannot raise capitalists' incomes expressed in stable values either immediately or later. Immediately after a wage reduction the volume of investment and capitalists' consumption remains unaltered, and thus so does the capitalists' income expressed in stable values. Employment does not alter, while all prices fall in the same proportion that wages have been reduced. Thus nothing is changed by wage reduction except the "general level" of prices, and thus there is no reason for capitalists to increase the volume of their consumption and investment later if they did not so at the beginning.[1]

Or, to put it in a different way: The volume of capitalists' consumption and investment is initially unchanged. Thus there is no increase in output and employment in the luxury and investment goods industries. It follows that the demand for wage-goods falls proportionately to wages, so that since prime costs are reduced also in the same proportion there is no change in the output of the wage-goods industry. Consequently output and employment in all three industries are unchanged and prices fall uniformly in the proportion of the wage reduction.

[1] I have already treated the problem of wages in this way in my article "Essai d'une Théorie du Mouvement Cycliques des Affaires," *Revue d'Economie Politique*, March–April 1935, pp. 301–2.

But then capitalists have no incentive to raise their consumption or investment, for their income expectations are not realized.

Since capitalists' consumption and investment do not increase immediately, their income is initially unchanged; since their income is initially unchanged, their consumption and investment and consequently their income also fails to increase later on.

IMPERFECT COMPETITION INTRODUCED

1. We are going now gradually to remove our assumptions. We drop first that of free competition and examine the relation between real wages and employment in a system such as described in the first essay, in which imperfect competition prevails and average wage-cost curves in the majority of enterprises are more or less horizontal. We have shown there (pp. 36–39): (1) That in such a system the ratio

$$\frac{\text{index of average wage cost}}{\text{index of prices of finished goods}}$$

is approximately constant; (2) that the index of average wage cost does not depend appreciably on the level of output and employment, and thus, with a constant technique and intensity of labour, the index of average wage-cost does not differ greatly from the index of wage rates; (3) that the index of prices of finished goods does not greatly deviate from that of the cost of living.

It follows from these three points that the index of real wages tends to be more or less stable provided the technique of production and intensity of labour do not alter. Consequently in actual fact the index of real wages must show a steady tendency to rise, since there is a strong secular trend in the productivity of labour due to improvements in technique and the increase in intensity of work. But if we eliminate the trend from the index of real wages, we can expect a series of great stability, though *some* fluctuations must be present, as both the technique of production and the intensity of labour may show some rather irregular changes apart from the secular trend, and in addition the ratio

$$\frac{\text{index of average wage cost}}{\text{index of prices of finished goods}}$$

is only approximately constant. (The small fluctuations in it depend partly, as we shall see, on changes in money wages.) To sum up, we should expect that in a closed system real wages, after the elimination of secular trend, would show relatively small changes which would not be likely to have any strong (positive or negative correlation) with the level of employment.

We shall use as a statistical illustration the data on real wages in the U.S.A.—which may be considered an approximately closed system—for the period 1919–35. We have computed for this purpose a combined index of hourly wages in the manufacturing, building, railroads, and agriculture, and divided it by an index of the cost of living.[1]

[1] We used the data on hourly (for agriculture monthly) wages, published in *Survey of Current Business*. The indices of wages of the four industries mentioned were weighted in proportion of their wage bills in 1929 as given in Dr. Kuznets's *National Income and Capital Formation, 1919–1935* (pp. 62, 63).

TABLE 7

Real Wages in the U.S.A.

1929 = 100

1919	81	1925	92	1931	108
1920	86	1926	92	1932	106
1921	87	1927	96	1933	109
1922	87	1928	98	1934	118
1923	91	1929	100	1935	117
1924	93	1930	103		

We see at a glance a strong trend, doubtless due to technical progress, etc., which amounts on an average to 2·25 per cent per year. The series obtained after eliminating the trend is given in Table 8, together with the index of output in the U.S.A. (gross national product at 1929 prices).[1]

TABLE 8

Real Wages after Elimination of Trend and Output in the U.S.A.

1929 = 100

	Real Wages	Output		Real Wages	Output
1919	100	71	1928	100	97
1920	103	73	1929	100	100
1921	102	69	1930	101	91
1922	100	74	1931	104	78
1923	103	82	1932	100	61
1924	103	83	1933	100	63
1925	100	86	1934	106	73
1926	98	92	1935	103	78
1927	100	92			

[1] Inclusive of repairs, Dr. Kuznets's *National Income and Gross Capital Formation*, pp. 8, 80.

The fluctuations in real wages are small, and it is easy to see that no clear negative or positive correlation with those of output exists. Real wages at the bottom of the slump (1932, 1933), e.g. are equal to those at the top of the boom (1928, 1929).

2. Let us next examine the process of wage reduction. So long as we assume that the degree of monopoly (i.e. the ratio of prices to marginal costs) remains unaltered, the effect of an all-round wage reduction is just the same as with perfect competition. For if it is assumed that the volume of capitalists' consumption and investment does not change immediately, there is initially no change in employment; while prices, since they change proportionately to prime costs, are in this case reduced proportionately to wages. But since the only change in the system is that in the "general price level," there will be no inducement for capitalists to increase their consumption and investment at a later date.

It is doubtful, however, whether the degree of monopoly really remains unaffected by the process of wage reduction. Some prices are likely to be "sticky," i.e. not to fall at all, or to fall less than marginal costs.[1] This has an important influence upon the result of a wage cut. The output of investment and luxury goods does not change immediately after a wage reduction (according to our fundamental assumption), and thus employment in the industries making these goods is unaltered. The money demand of workers is consequently

[1] See pp. 35–36.

reduced (as in the cases considered above) proportionately to wages, but the prices of wage-goods do not decline on the average to the same extent. As a result the "real" demand for wage-goods falls off, and so does the output and employment in the wage-goods industry. Thus, paradoxically, both employment and real wages are here reduced by the wage cut. And when this has occurred, there will still be no incentive for capitalists to increase their consumption and investment.

Indeed, as the volume of capitalists' consumption and investment is initially unaltered, capitalists' money income (being equal to the value of these two items) is reduced in the same proportion as the prices of luxury and investment goods. If the respective prices of these two types of goods are reduced roughly in the same proportion, the ratio of profits to the price of investment goods is unchanged, and so is also the profitability of new investment. Thus neither investment nor capitalists' consumption is encouraged at a later stage provided it did not rise at the beginning.

To sum up, any increase in the degree of monopoly due to a wage cut reduces employment, the real wage rate and (for both these reasons) the real wage bill, but it does not increase the capitalists' income expressed in stable values.

3. If the wage cut increases the degree of monopoly and thus reduces the relative share of manual labour in the national income, it may be asked how it is possible for this relative share to remain approximately stable throughout the business cycle. We have already stated

in the essay on "The Distribution of the National Income" that in a depression the degree of monopoly increases (because of wage reductions and for other reasons), but this adverse influence upon the share of manual labour is counterbalanced by the fall in raw material prices relative to wages (see pp. 36 sqq.). In the boom the reverse occurs.

As a result, the influence of a change in money wages upon real wages via the degree of monopoly is obscured and only sharp fluctuations in the former are reflected in the latter. This is illustrated by Table 9, in which have been computed the indices of money wages in the U.S.A. (the combined index of wage rates in agriculture, manufacturing, building, and railways used above) and real wages (the corresponding series after elimination of secular trend calculated above).

TABLE 9

Real Wages after Elimination of Trend and Money Wages in the U.S.A.

		1929 = 100			
	Money Wages	Real Wages		Money Wages	Real Wages
1919	83	100	1928	98	100
1920	102	103	1929	100	100
1921	89	102	1930	100	101
1922	84	100	1931	94	104
1923	91	103	1932	82	100
1924	95	103	1933	81	100
1925	96	100	1934	94	106
1926	96	98	1935	97	103
1927	98	100			

As we see, the fluctuations in money wages are much more violent than those in real wages. The "jumps" in the former (1919–20, 1920–21, 1931–32, 1933–34) are reflected on a much smaller scale by the latter.

FURTHER ASSUMPTIONS REMOVED

1. We have supposed so far that salary earners and manual workers do not save, and that the various types of salary and wage rates change always in the same proportion. We shall now make more reasonable assumptions.

We divide the salary earners into two categories, which we shall typify as "clerks" and "managers." We assume that the salary rates of the first group move proportionately to wage rates, and that both manual workers and "clerks" do not save (for their saving is in fact unimportant). However, we do allow for "managers" saving, and suppose their salaries to change in the same direction as capitalists' incomes, but in a lesser proportion.

The "balance sheet" of the national income can now be written as follows:

Capitalists' income	Investment
"Managers' " salaries	Consumption
Wages and "clerks' " salaries	

Since manual workers and "clerks" do not save, we obtain by subtracting their joint incomes from both sides

Capitalists' and "managers' " income = Investment
  + Capitalists' and "managers' " consumption

86

If the money income of "managers" always moved proportionately to that of capitalists, our previous argument on wage reduction would fully apply to the case now considered with this one change, that capitalists' and managers' income or consumption must be substituted for capitalists' income or consumption respectively.

But the fact that the income of "managers" varies to a lesser extent than that of capitalists' modifies to a certain degree the results of a wage cut. Indeed, the relative shift of income from capitalists' to "managers" increases their joint consumption, for the latter have a greater propensity to consume than the former (capitalists' incomes include the corporative saving). Thus employment is stimulated. On the other hand, this shift unfavourably affects the profitability of investment, and thus exerts a certain pressure on investment and consequently upon employment. On balance it is uncertain how employment will be affected, but the effect of the shift of income from capitalists to managers caused by wage reduction is not likely to be great.

2. A similar problem arises when we discard our assumption that the entrepreneurs and rentiers have an equal propensity to consume. In reality that of rentiers is usually higher because entrepreneurial incomes include the corporative saving. Thus when the total money income of capitalists declines as the result of a wage cut and the relative share of rentiers in it increases, the volume of capitalists' consumption tends to increase. And this consequently affects favourably total capitalists'

income (expressed in stable values) and employment. As a result also investment becomes more profitable, for (with a given rate of interest) the increased burden of payments to rentiers does not concern new investments, but only past ones. This in turn strengthens the tendency for employment and capitalists' income to rise. However, the change in capitalists' propensity to consume because of the shifts in the distribution of income between entrepreneurs and rentiers described above is not likely to be very important, and so its final effect must not be overestimated.[1]

3. We can now sum up the modifications introduced by passing from our simplified model towards real conditions.

(1) Real wages have no close (positive or negative) correlation with employment because in reality imperfect competition and more or less horizontal curves of average wage-cost prevail in the majority of enterprises.

(2) A wage cut tends to raise the degree of monopoly, and consequently to reduce real wages and to affect employment unfavourably.

(3) A wage cut causes a relative shift of income from capitalists to "managers." As a result, consumption tends to increase and investment to fall off. How it affects employment is uncertain, but the change in either direction is likely to be small.

(4) A wage cut causes also a relative shift of income

[1] The more so that as a result of the redistribution of capitalists' income the saving of enterprises is smaller in relation to total saving, and this tends to discourage investment. See below, p. 132.

from entrepreneurs to rentiers. This tends to increase capitalists' propensity to consume, and consequently employment and "real" capitalists' incomes.

On the balance we can say that:

(1) A wage reduction may change employment in either direction, but this change is likely to be small.

(2) It tends to redistribute income to the disadvantage of the workers. (The fall in real wages is, however, much smaller than that in money wages.)

Of course in the case of a rise in money wages the statements must be reversed.

4. One last assumption was still left unremoved; that of the rate of interest being kept constant. As we have seen, a wage cut does not cause any important change in employment and output, while prices decline. As a result, the value of output must diminish and the demand for cash for transactions fall off. Thus the rate of interest tends to decline, and this encourages investment so that we have yet another possible way for a wage cut to raise employment.

This argument, though theoretically quite correct, is, however, without practical importance. The increase in the demand for cash in general affects only slightly the long-term rate of interest, which is the most important rate in the determination of the level of investment.[1] Thus it seems to be quite justifiable to neglect this channel through which a wage reduction could influence the level of employment.

5. We gave above a statistical illustration of there

[1] See below, pp. 112–113.

being no close connection between real wages and employment and of the influence of change in money wages upon real wages. The effect of a change in money-wages on employment is much more difficult to trace statistically because the latter is usually subject to many other influences. In the slump, e.g., both wages and employment decline, which does not prove, however, that wage reductions depress employment.

A crucial test in which most of the irrelevant factors were absent was provided by the Blum Experiment. The detailed account of this investigation was published elsewhere,[1] and we will here refer only shortly to the chief conclusions.

In the article concerned we came to the conclusion that the results of the Blum Experiment (lasting from the spring of 1936 till the spring of 1937) were approximately equivalent to the consequences of an increase of wages in a closed economy by 60 per cent. It was further stated that this great change hardly affected output, and that real wages per hour rose by 26 per cent. (The long-term rate of interest was approximately stable.) This is in full accordance with the theory developed above. It must be noticed that some factors (e.g. Governmental control of rents, railway tariffs, prices of bread, etc.) strengthened the natural tendency of some prices to remain "sticky," and thus the rise in real wages was greater than if "natural" conditions had prevailed. (In other words, the fall in the degree of monopoly was unusually great.)

[1] *Economic Journal*, March 1938.

FINAL REMARKS

1. There are certain "workers' friends" who try to persuade the working class to abandon the fight for wages, of course in its own interest. The usual argument used for this purpose is that the increase of wages causes unemployment, and is thus detrimental to the working class as a whole.

The Keynesian theory undermines the foundation of this argument. Our investigation above has shown that a wage increase may change employment in either direction, but that this change is unlikely to be important. A wage increase, however, affects to a certain extent the distribution of income: it tends to reduce the degree of monopoly and thus to raise real wages. On the other hand, "real" capitalists' incomes tend to fall off because of the relative shift of income from rentiers to corporations which lowers the capitalists' propensity to consume.

If viewed from this standpoint, strikes must have the full sympathy of "workers' friends." For a rise in wages tends to reduce the degree of monopoly, and thus to bring our imperfect system nearer to the ideal of free competition. On the other hand, it tends to increase the thriftiness of capitalists by causing a relative shift of income from rentiers to corporations. And "workers' friends" are usually admirers both of free competition and of thrift as a virtue of the capitalist class.

2. Another question may arise in connection with the Keynesian theory of wages. Is not the struggle of workers for higher wages idle if they lose whatever gain they

91

may make in the form of a higher cost of living? We have shown that wage reduction causes a change in the distribution of the national income to the disadvantage of workers, and that in the event of an increase in wages the reverse occurs. This is not to deny, however, that changes in real wages are much smaller than those in money wages; but nevertheless they may be quite material; especially as we are dealing with averages which reflect only slightly great fluctuations in real wages in particular industries.

We noticed above the great stability of the relative share of manual labour in the national income. This is not in contradiction with the influence of money wages upon the distribution of the national income. On the contrary, the resistance to wage cut prevents the degree of monopoly from rising in the slump to the extent it would if "free competition" prevailed on the labour market. Though in fact the relative share of manual labour is more or less stable, this would not obtain if wages were very "elastic."

It is quite true that the fight for wages is not likely to bring about fundamental changes in the distribution of the national income. Income and capital taxation are much more potent weapons to achieve this aim, for these taxes (as opposed to commodity taxes) do not affect prime costs, and thus do not tend to raise prices. But in order to redistribute income in this way, the Government must have both the will and the power to carry it out, and this is unlikely in a capitalist system.

Part Two

4

THE PRINCIPLE OF INCREASING RISK[1]

THE PROBLEM

1. The subject of this essay is the determination of the amount of investment undertaken at a given time by a single entrepreneur. He intends, for instance, to build a factory for the production of a certain product. He is faced with given market conditions: he knows the price of the product in question, the level of wages and the prices of raw materials, the cost of construction and the rate of interest. Besides, he has some rather vague ideas as to the probable future change in prices and costs. This knowledge is the basis for the planning of investment, i.e. for the choice of the amount of capital k (measured in terms of money) to be invested and the method of production to be applied.

With a *given* amount of capital k and a given method of production the entrepreneur is able to estimate the series of future returns (differences between revenues and effective costs) $q_1, q_2 . . q_n$ during the prospective life of the factory. We shall call the rate ϵ at which the series of returns must be discounted in order to obtain the amount invested k, the prospective rate of profit,[2]

[1] This essay is an altered version of the article published in *Economica*, November 1937.

[2] This definition corresponds to Professor Fisher's "rate of return over cost," Mr. Boulding's "internal rate of return," and Mr. Keynes's "marginal efficiency of capital."

while by prospective profit π we mean the product $k \cdot \epsilon$. Now we can assume that with a given amount to invest k the entrepreneur will choose such a method of production as will maximize the prospective rate of profit, or, what amounts to the same (k being given), the prospective profit $\pi = k\epsilon$. Thus to every value of k there corresponds a definite maximum prospective profit π_m.

The method of production having been chosen for each value of k, the entrepreneur has still to decide on the optimum k, i.e. the size of investment. He must charge the capital invested at the market rate of interest ρ and also make some allowance for risk, the rate of which we denote by σ. Thus the entrepreneur's prospective gain g is:

$$g = \pi_m - (\rho + \sigma)k$$

The entrepreneur will obtain the maximum gain at the value of k which satisfies the equation

$$\frac{d\pi_m}{dk} = \rho + \sigma$$

and this value of k is the optimum amount of investment. Now $\frac{d\pi_m}{dk}$ is simply the prospective rate of profit of a small capital addition dk to the amount invested k, supposing that both k and $k + dk$ are invested with the appropriate optimum method of production. We shall call $\frac{d\pi_m}{dk}$ marginal prospective rate of profit, or for the sake of brevity marginal rate of profit. We can consequently say that the size of investment k_0 is determined by that level at which the marginal rate of profit is equal to the sum of the rate of interest ρ and rate of risk σ. (See Fig. 6.)

2. It can easily be seen from the chart that the

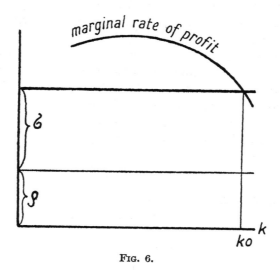

FIG. 6.

optimum amount k_0 to be invested is finite only if the marginal rate of profit falls when k exceeds a certain value. It is commonly believed that such a fall does in fact occur, and for two reasons: (1) large-scale diseconomies; (2) imperfect competition. The first reason seems to be unrealistic. Clearly it has no technological basis. True, every machine has an optimum size, but why not have ten (or more) machines of this type?

97   G

There remains the argument of difficulties of management arising out of large-scale enterprise. But this also is doubtful (why not start ten factories instead of one with ten independent directors?), and anyway could apply only to industrial giants far above the average size of existing enterprises.

The second reason for the limited size of investment is quite realistic, but does not cover the ground fully. The effect of imperfect competition in limiting the amount of investment k may often be overcome by spreading the latter over various fields: imperfect competition then operates to limit the portion of k invested in any particular field, but not to limit the total amount of k. On the other hand, imperfect competition cannot account for the fact that in a given industry at the same time large and small enterprises are started. Thus there must be yet another factor restricting the size of an investment.

INCREASING RISK

1. We have assumed so far—as is usually done—that the rate of risk is independent of the amount invested k. It is this assumption which has to be dropped, I think, in order to obtain a realistic solution of the problem of limited investment. It is reasonable to assume that marginal risk increases with the amount invested. For the greater the investment the greater is the reduction of the entrepreneur's income from his own capital when the average rate of profit falls short of the rate of interest. Suppose the rate of interest is 5 per cent, the entre-

preneur's own capital £1,000,000, and the credit taken also £1,000,000. If the average rate of return is only 3 per cent, the total income of the entrepreneur is £10,000 as compared with £30,000 if he had borrowed nothing; while with £2,000,000 credit he suffers a net loss of £10,000, which, if it continues long enough, will drive him into bankruptcy.

If, however, the entrepreneur is not cautious enough in his investment activity, it is the creditor who imposes on his calculation the burden of increasing risk, charging the successive portions of credits above a certain amount with a rising rate of interest.[1]

The amount invested k_0 is now given by the condition of the marginal rate of profit being equal to the sum of the marginal rate of risk σ and the rate of interest ρ. The $\rho + \sigma$ curve is not a horizontal curve as in Fig. 6, *but an upward sloping one.* The point of its intersection with the marginal rate of profit curve determines the amount of the investment in the absence of large-scale diseconomies and imperfect competition (Fig. 7).

Now the various sizes of enterprises started in the same industry at a given time can be easily explained. The smaller the private capital of an entrepreneur investing an amount k the greater the risk of impairing his income. Thus the smaller the private capital the higher is the $\rho + \sigma$ curve, and—as is easy to see from the chart—

---

[1] See M. Breit, "Ein Beitrag zur Theorie der Geld-und Kapitalmarktes," *Zeitschrift fuer Nationaloekonomie*, Band VI, Heft 5, p. 641. The principle of increasing risk is a generalization of Mr. Breit's ideas.

the smaller the amount invested k_0. The enterprises started in a given industry at a given moment are not of equal size because the private capital of the various entrepreneurs is not the same. "Business democracy" is a fallacy: the amount of the entrepreneur's private capital is a "factor of investment."

2. Legitimate doubt may arise as to whether the

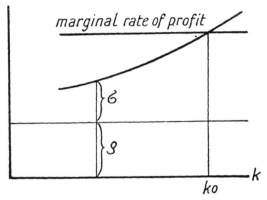

FIG. 7.

results arrived at above are applicable to the case of joint-stock companies. If a company issues bonds or debentures the situation is not materially altered. The greater the issue the more are dividends impaired in the event of unsuccessful business. The position is also similar in the case of an issue of preference shares (the fixed interest on which is paid from profit before dividends on ordinary shares are distributed). But what about an issue of ordinary shares? *Prima facie* it would

100

seem that no limits are set to such an issue, but in fact this is not the case. It is clear that the shareholders of an existing company or the promoters of a new one have no reason whatsoever to grant to new shareholders the full rate of profit from the investment undertaken: on the contrary, they will keep back a part for themselves either by accepting bonus shares, or by issuing the new shares above par and adding the agio gains to reserves. But a limit is set to these efforts to "cheapen" the capital received from new shareholders by the fact that the narrower is the margin between the prospective dividend on new shares and the rate of interest the smaller will be the market for the new shares. Thus there exists an "optimum size" of issue which is relatively small. (Even if the company tries to increase it by "exaggerating" the prospects of the enterprise the limit is set by the cost of advertisement and kindred "services.") This explains the fact that issues of ordinary shares do not play at all a very important part as compared with issues of bonds and preference shares.

The fundamental factors determining the optimum size of an issue of ordinary shares are essentially the same as in the case of floating a loan: the prospective rate of profit and the rate of interest. But their influence is here exerted in a much more complicated way, and may be distorted by speculative demand for shares which is often only loosely connected with the actual profitability of the enterprise. However, it seems justifiable to assume as a first approximation that conditions of investment activity are such as would

101

obtain if all finance was by way of loans; this the more so, because, as mentioned above, ordinary shares do not play a very important part in the finance of investment.

THE RATE OF INTEREST AND THE METHOD OF PRODUCTION

1. In the case represented in Fig. 7 we have constant returns and imperfect competition is abstracted. Though in the general case Fig. 6 there corresponds to each point on the marginal rate of profit curve a different method of production, it is clear that with constant returns and perfect competition technique does not change with the amount invested: the maximum rate of profit is obtained by the application of the same method of production, whatever the scale of enterprise.

Let us now consider what happens if the rate of interest is lowered. The $\rho + \sigma$ curve shifts down, and its point of intersection with the marginal efficiency curve moves to the right (Fig. 8). The method of production chosen by the entrepreneur in his plan does not change as the size of investment increases. *Consequently so long as constant returns prevail and we abstract the influence of imperfect competition the change in the rate of interest does not affect the method of production chosen by the entrepreneur, but only the size of the investment planned.*

2. This statement seems to be in contradiction with the classical theory of marginal productivity of capital and labour, but the contradiction is only apparent. The

point of departure of the classical doctrine is a drastically simplified model of production in which the quantity of product is a definite function of the amount of "real" capital and labour used. A necessary condition of long-run equilibrium is equality between the marginal productivity of each factor and its price divided by the price of product. In the case of constant returns (homo-

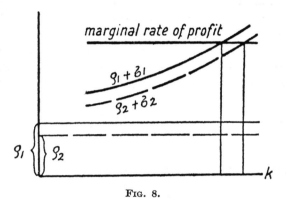

FIG. 8.

geneous production function) this is also a *sufficient* condition for long-run equilibrium, for with constant returns the marginal productivity equations exclude the existence of entrepreneurial gain. If the rate of interest falls, a shift towards a new long-run equilibrium must take place in which the marginal productivity of capital is lower, that of labour higher, and more capital is used in proportion to labour. But the theory says nothing about the immediate influence of a fall in the rate of interest on the plans of the entrepreneur. Such

103

a fall in the case of constant returns (if our principle of increasing risk is not taken into account) must create a tendency to plan investment of infinite size and with an indefinite method of production.[1]

However, after the output of the product has suddenly increased, its price falls, and this makes possible the restoration of another long-run equilibrium in which the marginal productivity equations are satisfied.[2]

Thus our problem was quite different from that of classical theory. We examined the planning of the entrepreneur in a given situation which in general was *not* the position of long-run equilibrium. We tried to find the factor limiting the size of the investment planned, and this factor, as we see, is non-existent in the classical theory in the case of firms subject to constant returns and not in the position of long-run equilibrium. And our statement that the fall in the rate of interest does not affect the method of production, but only the scale of investment plans, referred only to the *plans* and not to the situation arising out of their realization.

The classical thesis that a low rate of interest causes the use of more capitalistic method of production was

[1] It is sometimes considered obvious that the method of production is chosen so as to minimize average costs. This assumption, however, attributes to the entrepreneur the tendency to maximize the profit per unit of output, while he of course tends to attain the maximum total profit. Both tendencies are equivalent only if a given output is planned.

[2] This treatment is, however, very formal, for in reality an upward self-stimulating process begins which causes (if the rate of interest is not raised) either hyperinflation or fluctuations about the new position of long-run equilibrium.

often applied not only to the long-run equilibrium position, but also to entrepreneurs' planning in "disequilibrium." This interpretation is of course wrong, and, as we have shown above, if we abstract imperfect competition and introduce the principle of increasing risk, the fall in the rate of interest has no immediate effect on the method of production decided upon by entrepreneurs in making their plans.[1]

"COMMITMENTS" AS A FUNCTION OF MARGINAL NET PROFITABILITY

So far we have dealt with the investment of a firm starting afresh, with a given capital of its own. This is of course a special case. In general investments undertaken by firms are not their "maiden" ones. The burden of risk borne by a firm does not depend solely on investment currently planned. This burden is the result of all its "commitments," by which term we mean here all its investments past and present minus its own (present) capital. Thus its "commitments" are equal to the cost of the past investment constituting its capital equipment plus investment orders in execution, or recently given, minus private capital consisting of the firm's own capital

---

[1] It may be shown, however, that if imperfect competition is operative, the decline in the rate of interest exerts some influence towards more capitalistic methods of production in investment plans. This different effect of increasing risk and imperfect competition upon the method of production depends on the fact that the marginal risk increases with the amount of *capital* invested, while the marginal revenue falls with the increase in *output*.

at the start, and the amounts accumulated since (inclusive of amortization). If, e.g., the cost of the capital equipment of a firm is £1,000,000, the investment orders in execution £100,000, the investment orders given to-day £50,000, while the original capital of the firm and the amount accumulated since (inclusive of the amortization fund), £800,000; the "commitments" of this firm are

$$£1,000,000 + £100,000 + £50,000 - £800,000 = £350,000$$

Now it is easy to see that in general it is to the total amount of "commitments" that the curve of increasing risk relates. The investment plans undertaken to-day must be such as to "push" commitments to the point at which marginal risk is equal to the difference between the marginal rate of profit and the rate of interest. Or if we call this difference the marginal net profitability, we can say that the "commitments" of a firm are an increasing function of the marginal net profitability.[1]

It is important to notice that if a firm's investment in a certain period is equal to its saving, its commitments are unaltered, and the marginal risk incurred is not increased.

The connection due to increasing risk, between commitments and net profitability, plays an important part in the theory of business cycle developed in the last essay.

[1] If we consider a long period in which the proportionate rise of the private capital of the firm may be substantial, it is really the ratio of "commitments" to private capital which is the function of the marginal net profitability.

5

THE LONG-TERM RATE OF INTEREST

THE FINANCE OF INVESTMENT

We propose in this essay to analyse briefly the monetary phenomena accompanying investment in fixed capital equipment. In particular we intend to examine the influence of the latter upon the long-term rate of interest, and also to explain the remarkable stability of this rate.

We assume throughout the essay a closed economic system.

Liabilities of the Banks are regarded as being composed of Deposits on which interest is paid and Current Accounts on which none is paid, while assets consist of Notes, Bills, Bonds, and Advances. The ratio of Notes to Liabilities is kept more or less constant. The Central Bank is supposed to behave as in Great Britain, i.e. to supply the economy with cash by buying bills and bonds on the market.

2. We shall first consider the financing of investment in fixed capital under simplifying assumptions which will eventually be removed. We assume for the time being: (1) that on each day of the construction period of a given object of investment bank advances are taken to the extent of the expenditure made during the day; (2) that on the next day a loan of the same amount

is floated and the advance of the preceding day repaid; (3) that savings accumulated in any one day are used in the next to buy bonds.

What will happen under these conditions if additional investment is undertaken can easily be seen. Since saving is equal to investment, to-day's additional accumulation of savings on current accounts equals advances taken for additional investment. To-morrow the flotation of loans to the amount of to-day's investment will be met out of to-day's savings. In this way an increase in the rate of investment will directly result in only a negligible addition to the advances and current accounts of the banks.

The increase in the rate of investment, however, brings about a rise of output in both investment and consumption goods industries, and this creates a greater demand for money for transactions. Current accounts and advances tend to increase, and the banks are obliged to sell bills and bonds in order to be able to expand their credits.

We will consider the results of these sales in detail later on, but first we shall remove our simplifying assumptions and thus show other factors tending to intensify the pressure on the bill and bond market.

3. We suppose now that, instead of financing construction day by day with advances for one day only, the cost of a given object of investment is advanced *en bloc* at the time when its construction is begun. A deposit account (of the same amount as the total cost of the investment object) is opened, out of which the

expenditure on construction is financed. We shall call this account the "investment finance fund."[1] It diminishes gradually as construction proceeds, and is fully spent when the object of investment is finished. (Thus the average period of turnover of the "investment finance fund" is half the construction period.)

The sums spent on construction create equal amounts of saving, which, let us suppose, are accumulated for the time being also on the deposit account, and which are consequently equal in value at the end of construction to the total credit advanced. The loan then floated in order to fund this credit is exactly taken up by the accumulated savings. We shall call the savings which accumulate on deposit account the "intermediate savings fund." Its average period of turnover is also half the construction period.

Now it is easy to see that if the money value of the rate of investment in fixed capital I_m prevails at a certain level and the average construction period is θ, the bank advances for construction must be equal to $I_m \cdot \theta$. And on deposit accounts there is an "investment finance fund and an "intermediate savings fund," each of the value $I_m \cdot \dfrac{\theta}{2}$. If I_m increases, all these items rise proportionately.

It must be added that the above representation is based on the assumption that the time-lag in directing savings towards the purchase of securities is just half the construction period. If it is not, certain complications

---

[1] It is this fund which has been called by Keynes "finance."

arise which, however, do not materially affect our result, and thus we abstract them from our argument.

4. We see now that if investment in fixed capital increases, bank advances tend to rise, not only because of the increase in the demand for money for transactions, but also because the "investments finance fund" and "intermediate saving fund" are expanding. In this way additional pressure is exerted on the banks to sell bills and bonds. Before we start to consider the influence of this pressure upon the rate of interest, we must remove another simplification involved in the above argument.

We have supposed so far throughout the argument that new savings are (with a certain delay) fully used for the purchase of securities. It is quite possible, however, that they may be devoted partly for the repayment of advances (or what amounts to the same thing in periods of increasing activity when the demand for money for transactions rises they are left on current account while advances increase *pro tanto* less). This, however, does not materially affect the course of our argument. A part of the loans floated is then not taken up by savers, but the banks are *pro tanto* relieved from advances and enabled to take up loans instead. Here, however, a complication arises, since in general banks use the amounts released by repayment of advances partly for the purchase of bills and not of bonds. As a result, the pressure on the bill market is relieved, and that on the bond market *pro tanto* strengthened.

THE INFLUENCE UPON THE RATES OF INTEREST

1. We stated above that an increase in investment causes the banks to sell bills and bonds in order to be able to expand advances. If we ignore for a moment that a part of this supply may be purchased by the Central Bank, the only possible eventual buyers are the owners of deposits and current accounts. Let us first consider how this works as regards bills.

The sales of bills increase of course the discount rate, and this makes bills more attractive to the potential buyers. But it is easy to show that the demand for them is rather inelastic. Indeed, the most likely buyers are the owners of deposits, for the latter bear more or less the character of reserves. The rate paid on the deposits, however, moves usually parallel to the discount rate, and thus there is no change in comparative advantage. Therefore the bills must eventually be bought by the owners of current accounts. The higher rate of discount induces people to manage their transactions with smaller amounts of money, and thus enables some bills to be bought (or permits repayment of advances, the rate on which moves parallel to the rate of discount; and so reduces the sales of bills by banks). It is clear, however, that in order to produce this effect the change in the rate of discount must be appreciable.

Of course the Central Bank in buying bills reduces very much the pressure of sales. For banks may obtain in this way additional amounts of notes, and this enables them to expand credit by, say, £10 for each £1 note obtained. But the effect of the Central Bank's buying is

111

partly counterbalanced by the fact that with increasing activity the demand for notes "in circulation" rises. At any rate there is an inherent tendency in the system for strong fluctuations in the discount rate, which in fact often makes itself felt.

2. What, however, about the sale of bonds? It is known that their yields fluctuate much less than the discount rate. Why do sales of bonds taking place together with sales of bills depress only slightly the long-term rate of interest? This, I think, is due to the fact that many of the deposit owners are willing to buy bonds when their yield increases in spite of the much greater increase in the rate on deposits. (If, e.g., the long-term rate increases from 4 to 4·2, while the rate on deposits from 2 to 3.) The reason for such behaviour on the part of this type of deposit owners is as follows:

Consider a capitalist with a "non-speculative outlook," who faces the alternatives of holding his reserves in bonds or deposits. There is the advantage of a stable and generally higher income on the side of bonds: on the other hand, deposits are constant in value, while the price of bonds, in the case of an emergency which may necessitate their sale in the indefinite future cannot be foreseen, and the risk of loss is always present. Thus it is clear that the stimulus to keep bonds is the margin between the *present* long-term rate and the anticipated *average* short-term rate over a long period. Now it is very likely that the change in the present rate on deposits does not greatly affect the expectations of its average over a long period. Thus it is plausible that a deposit owner of the type considered may be induced to buy bonds though the rate on deposits has increased much more than the yield of bonds.

STATISTICAL ILLUSTRATION AND GENERAL REMARKS

1. The relative stability of the long-term rate of interest is generally known. But perhaps it is not fully realized how small are in fact its "purely cyclical" fluctuations. This can be seen from the table on p. 114, in which we have computed the difference between the yield of Consols and the 9-year moving average for the period 1853–1932.[1]

Only in the World War, early post-war years, and 1932 does the "cyclical deviation" of the long-term rate of interest exceed 0·2.

These facts are of great importance in the investigation of the business cycle. It seems likely that changes in the long-term rate of interest of the order of those noticed, say from 3·0 to 3·2, can hardly influence investment activity[2] to a great extent. Thus it will be a justifiable simplification if we assume in the analysis of the business cycle that the long-term rate of interest is constant. This assumption may be contested on the ground that it is the yield of industrial bonds which matters in investment activity, and that this yield increases (sometimes appreciably) in deep depressions because of

---

[1] The yields of Consols over the period considered are taken from the article "The Future of the Rate of Interest," J. Stafford, *The Manchester School*, VIII, No. 2, p. 137.

[2] See for that point Harrod, *The Trade Cycle*, p. 112.

the decline in lenders' confidence. The omission of this factor, however, does not distort the picture of the business cycle because it works in the same direction as the fall of the rate of profit, and therefore only aggra-

TABLE 10

Deviations of the yield of Consols from the 9-year moving average

1853	− 0·11	1873	+ 0·04	1893	+ 0·08	1913	− 0·16
54	+ 0·11	74	+ 0·05	94	+ 0·04	14	− 0·28
55	+ 0·14	75	+ 0·03	95	− 0·06	15	− 0·07
56	+ 0·04	76	− 0·02	96	− 0·14	16	+ 0·18
57	+ 0·06	77	− 0·01	97	− 0·18	17	+ 0·28
58	− 0·13	78	+ 0·03	98	− 0·16	18	− 0·06
59	− 0·07	79	− 0·01	99	− 0·10	19	+ 0·06
60	− 0·03	80	− 0·01	1900	+ 0·02	20	+ 0·70
61	+ 0·04	81	− 0·04	01	+ 0·10	21	+ 0·57
62	− 0·02	82	− 0·03	02	+ 0·02	22	− 0·21
63	− 0·03	83	− 0·04	03	+ 0·04	23	− 0·35
64	+ 0·06	84	+ 0·02	04	+ 0·07	24	− 0·26
65	+ 0·07	85	+ 0·12	05	− 0·04	25	− 0·12
66	+ 0·13	86	+ 0·12	06	− 0·04	26	+ 0·07
67	− 0·06	87	+ 0·12	07	+ 0·04	27	+ 0·13
68	− 0·09	88	− 0·18	08	− 0·08	28	− 0·05
69	− 0·03	89	− 0·12	09	− 0·07	29	+ 0·08
70	0·00	90	− 0·05	10	− 0·02	30	0·00
71	+ 0·01	91	+ 0·04	11	− 0·04	31	+ 0·08
72	+ 0·03	92	+ 0·10	12	− 0·07	32	− 0·37

vates the crises, but is not of fundamental importance for the mechanism of the trade cycle.

2. The fact of the stability of the long-term rate of interest stated above is particularly important for the analysis of the last stage of the boom. It excludes these theories of the business cycle which attribute the break-

down of prosperity to the increase of the rate of interest. For the rate of interest can stop the boom only by hampering investment, and it is chiefly the long-term rate which matters in investment activity.

Moreover, the fact of the stability of the long-term rate of interest shows indirectly that the boom ends in general before full employment is reached. When the system comes to the point of full employment, wages must rise sharply. But as shown above, this does not tend to reduce employment directly (see p. 89). Thus wages and prices continue to climb up, the demand for bank advances steadily increases, causing a strong rise in the short-term rate and—at least after a certain time —an appreciable increase in the long-term rate. Only this can overcome "inflation" by hampering investment and stopping the rise in wages and prices.

Since, however, no appreciable rise in the rate of interest usually occurs in the boom, it can be concluded that something like full employment is approached only in exceptional cases. In general unemployment (manifest or disguised) is sufficient to permit the boom to develop, and it is not the scarcity of labour which brings it to an end.

6

A THEORY OF THE BUSINESS CYCLE[1]

METHODOLOGICAL REMARKS AND SIMPLIFYING ASSUMPTIONS

1. The character of this essay is to a great extent different from that of the preceding ones. In the latter we frequently used simplified models, but only in order to solve some basic problems in their pure form, returning afterwards to the complexities of the real world. Here, however, we confine ourselves to the consideration of the business cycle only under simplifying assumptions, some of which may seem drastic. This is partly due to the peculiar character of the subject. The business cycle as such exists only as a tendency which in conjunction with what we call more or less vaguely "secular trend," "structural changes," etc., creates the extremely complex dynamic process we observe in the real world. Thus to pass from a simplified model to reality is to undertake a thorough analysis of this process as a whole, which is clearly beyond the scope of this essay.

[1] This essay is an altered version of the article published in *Review of Economic Studies*, February 1937. The essential ideas in it were developed already in my "Essai d'une Théorie du Mouvement Cyclique des Affaires," *Revue d'Economie Politique*, March–April 1935, and in mathematical form in "A Macrodynamic Theory of the Business Cycle," *Econometrica*, July 1935.

We cannot even find consolation in the idea that the mechanism of the business cycle, which we attempt here to construct, may be simply superimposed on the "secular trend," etc. On the contrary, the latter certainly affects the course of the business cycle as such.

This does not mean, however, that the consideration of the trade cycle in simplified models is a waste of time. To approach the dynamic process in all its complexity is certainly a hopeless task; so that the first step must consist in constructing elementary mechanisms of the "business cycle" or "secular trend." Only it must be kept in mind that these simple schemes are the beginning and not the end of economic dynamics.

2. We make the following simplifying assumptions. (1) We assume a closed economic system and a balanced State budget.[1] (2) We suppose the increase or decline in the volume of inventories (working capital and stocks) to be negligible. (3) We are dealing with an economy with no secular trend. The first assumption makes both the balance of expenditure of foreign countries and that of the Government equal to zero. Consequently investment I (as defined on p. 48), which is equal to private saving S, now becomes identical with private investment in fixed capital, working capital, and stocks. Thus bringing in assumption (2) about the constancy of inventories, we shall have in our model the equality between investment I and the output of fixed capital

[1] The doles for unemployed are financed by taxation or by the reduction of other State expenditure.

117

equipment.[1] However, before we proceed further, some explanation of the assumptions (2) and (3) is necessary.

3. There are various reasons why we abstract changes in inventories from our argument. The statistical evidence on this subject is very poor: the only series ranging over many years is that constructed by Dr. Kuznets for the U.S.A. during the period 1919–35.[2]

Except for this, we know very little about changes in inventories; while our knowledge of fluctuations in output of fixed capital equipment is considerably greater. (Steel production—the data on which are accessible for many countries over long periods—is a good indicator of the general output of fixed capital.)

Further, if we look at the changes in inventories and private investment in fixed capital in the U.S.A. in the period mentioned (see Fig. 9), we see at a glance that the former series is much less regular than the latter: indeed, one cannot properly speak of regular cyclical fluctuations in the changes in inventories. Nor is this surprising, for the latter are influenced by factors which are much more heterogeneous than those affecting investment in fixed capital. It follows that it is difficult to account for changes in inventories in a simple scheme, and, further, that they are not of primary importance in the explanation of the trade cycle. So far we have shown the desirability of keeping the changes in inven-

[1] Equipment in the course of construction is here *not* included in inventories. The change in the volume of equipment in the course of construction is contained in the "output of fixed capital equipment."

[2] *National Income and Gross Capital Formation, 1919–1935*, p. 40.

118

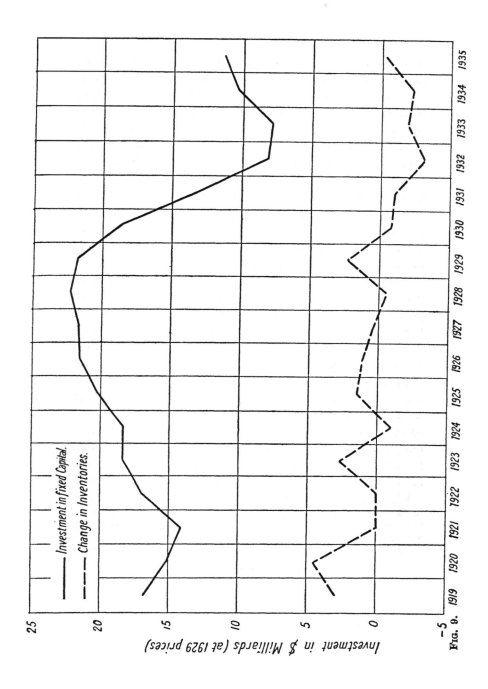

Investment in $ Milliards (at 1929 prices)

—— Investment in Fixed Capital.
– – – Change in Inventories.

FIG. 9.

tories out of our model. But how to "remove" them? i.e. how to construct our model in such a way as to keep the volume of inventories constant?

It is sometimes thought that the volume of inventories tends to vary proportionately with output, on the assumption that inventories are identical with working capital, which is regarded as bearing a constant relation

TABLE 11

The Volume of Inventories and Output in the U.S.A.

1929 = 100

	Inventories	Output		Inventories	Output
1919	72	71	1928	98	97
1920	81	73	1929	100	100
1921	87	69	1930	102	91
1922	87	74	1931	100	78
1923	90	82	1932	95	61
1924	92	83	1933	89	63
1925	93	86	1934	83	73
1926	96	92	1935	80	78
1927	98	92			

to output. Neither assumption is correct. Inventories contain besides working capital *sensu stricto* "stocks" in the form either of reserves or of accumulated unsold goods; and these move often in the opposite direction to working capital. Further working cápital in trade— in particular in the retail trade changes much more slower than sales; for dealers during a depression try to attract custom by stocking a greater variety of goods. As a result the volume of inventories is much more stable than that of output. On the basis of Dr. Kuznets'

120

data on changes in inventories and of the level of inventories in 1922 as given by Census of Production, we have computed the *level* of inventories in U.S.A. in the period 1919–35 (at 1929 prices).[1]

We see that inventories are very "sticky"; it is, for instance, surprising to learn that their volume in 1932 was only slightly lower than in 1928. Now one can easily imagine an economic system in which this tendency operates to the point of almost full stability of working capital and stocks, each fluctuating to the same extent but in opposite directions. Such a state of affairs need not seem fantastic in the light of the above figures.

4. We are next going to make some comments on the assumption of a "trendless" economy. We mean by this a system which can attain a state of long-run equilibrium, i.e. that there exists some position at which no change whatsoever occurs in the system.

It is clear that we cannot simply postulate a "trendless" economy, but we must attribute to our system characteristics which will render it trendless. This will be done largely in the course of the argument. At present we make only the following assumption. We suppose that not only manual workers (see p. 51) but also salary earners and rentiers do no saving. Obviously a contrary state of affairs is incompatible with "trendless" economy. Indeed, if salary earners and rentiers do save they may be expected in view of the relative stability

[1] Exclusive of the estimated value of movable equipment under construction, which we consider as fixed capital.

of their income to make some positive net saving in all circumstances. This, however, makes impossible the existence of a long-run equilibrium. For in such a state not only must there be no net saving, but in addition the net saving of salary earners and rentiers on the one hand and that of entrepreneurs on the other must each be equal to zero. For otherwise a shift of capital from entrepreneurs to salary earners and rentiers would take place, which would change the economic situation quite appreciably, as we shall see below (see p. 132).

Thus, if we want to deal with a "trendless" economy we must assume that all saving is done by entrepreneurs.

ASSUMPTIONS RESTATED

1. The consequences of our assumptions so far established are as follows:

(1) In our system the sole type of investment is private expenditure on fixed capital equipment (the consequence of the assumptions of a closed system, a balanced budget, and constant inventories).

(2) The workers and rentiers are supposed not to save, and thus all saving is done by entrepreneurs (the necessary conditions of a trendless economy).

2. Besides these assumptions, some of the conclusions of the preceding essays are used.

On the basis of the first essay we take for granted that the prices of finished investment goods change more or less proportionately to those of consumption goods (see pp. 37–40).

The argument of the second essay (p. 60) enables us

to assume that capitalists' incomes are determined by the national income Y (both expressed in stable values). We shall also use the equation established there (p. 67).

$$Y = f(I_{t-\lambda}) \quad . \quad . \quad . \quad . \quad . \quad (10)$$

which describes the functional relation between the national income Y at time t and investment I at time $t - \lambda$ (both expressed in stable values).

Further, we shall use the connection between the level of "commitments" contracted by entrepreneurs and the difference between the marginal rate of profit and the rate of interest—which was developed in the fourth essay (on the basis of the principle of increasing risk).

Lastly, in accordance with the results arrived at in the fifth essay, the long-term rate of interest will be assumed stable throughout the cycle.

INVESTMENT DECISIONS AND INVESTMENT

1. Investment in our model is solely in fixed capital, i.e. deliveries of finished capital goods plus the increase in fixed capital in the course of construction (the latter was *not* included in inventories). Thus investment is here equivalent to the work actually performed in the industries producing fixed capital equipment. And I (expressed in stable values) is equal to the volume of their output.[1]

---

[1] In the second essay in order to express investment, saving (which is equal to the former), and national income in stable values, we divided them by the index of prices of all finished

2. Since investment coincides in our system with the output of fixed capital, its actual level at any time is the result of past investment decisions which objectively took the form of orders for machines, buildings, etc.

Let us consider first the connection between the flow

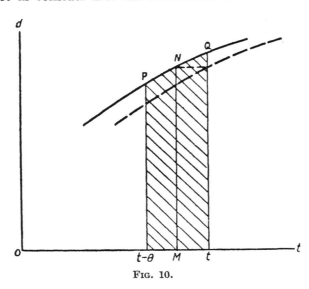

Fig. 10.

of decisions—orders for, and of output of, a particular type of investment goods. We denote the rate of investment orders for this type of goods by d, the output in

goods. Since, however, prices of finished investment goods (fixed capital equipment) and prices of finished consumption goods (cost of living) move almost proportionately (see pp. 37–40), I expressed in stable values coincides practically with the volume of output of investment goods industries.

the industry constructing them by i, and the construction period by θ.

All orders in the process of execution at the time t (Fig. 10) were given in the period from $t - \theta$ to t for previous orders were completed before $t - \theta$, while orders given after $t - \theta$ are still unfinished at time t. The volume of these outstanding orders is represented by the shaded area.

On the other hand, since all orders must be executed within a time θ, work corresponding to $\dfrac{1}{\theta}$ of each of the orders under execution must be performed per unit of time by the investment goods industry under consideration. And since the volume of all outstanding orders is given by the shaded area, the output i in this industry at the time t is equal to:

$$i = \frac{\text{shaded area}}{\theta}$$

It is easy to see from the diagram that this quotient is approximately equal to the median line MN. (This equality is perfect if PQ is a straight line.) Consequently the output i of our industry at time t is approximately equal to the rate of investment orders at the time $t - \dfrac{\theta}{2}$. Or the time-lag between d and i is approximately equal to half the construction period.

3. In reality we have of course not one type of investment goods, but many types with different construction periods. We shall call the volume of all types of investment orders per unit of time the rate of investment

decisions D; and the volume of the output of all types of fixed capital the rate of investment I.

The construction period of the various types of investment goods are different, but we can define the average construction period $\bar{\theta}$ as the ratio of the volume of all investment orders under execution (at a certain moment) to the total output of investment goods I. The average construction period is not constant, but if the distribution of orders between different types of investment does not undergo very great changes, which seems to be the case, variations in $\bar{\theta}$ will be slight. We shall assume that $\bar{\theta}$ is constant.

The argument developed in the preceding paragraph for d, i, and θ also applies approximately for D, I, and $\bar{\theta}$, and thus the time-lag between the rate of investment decisions and the output of investment goods is approximately equal to $\dfrac{\bar{\theta}}{2}$. Consequently we have that investment at time t is equal to the rate of investment decisions at time $t - \dfrac{\bar{\theta}}{2}$.

$$I_t = D_{t-\frac{\bar{\theta}}{2}} \quad . \quad . \quad . \quad . \quad . \quad (12)$$

(The available statistics show that the average construction period is probably between half a year and a year; thus $\dfrac{\bar{\theta}}{2}$ may be regarded as 3–6 months.)

4. We established in the second essay (p. 67) that the national income Y and investment I are connected by the equation

$$Y_t = f(I_{t-\lambda}) \quad . \quad . \quad . \quad . \quad . \quad (10)$$

126

Since investment at time $t - \lambda$ must be equal to the rate of investment decisions at time $t - \lambda - \dfrac{\bar{\theta}}{2}$, we have:

$$Y_t = f(D_{t - \lambda - \frac{\bar{\theta}}{2}}) \quad . \quad . \quad . \quad . \quad (13)$$

This means that since national income is lagging behind investment by λ and investment behind investment decisions by $\dfrac{\bar{\theta}}{2}$, income is lagging behind investment decisions by $\lambda + \dfrac{\bar{\theta}}{2}$. If we denote $\lambda + \dfrac{\bar{\theta}}{2}$ by τ we can write the last equation in the form:

$$Y_t = f(D_{t - \tau}) \quad . \quad . \quad . \quad . \quad (13a)$$

It may be mentioned that if we take $\dfrac{\bar{\theta}}{2}$ as 3–6 months and λ (see p. 73) as 4 months, τ amounts to 7–10 months.

The equation (13a) has important implications. It shows that past investment decisions determine the present national income, which of course influences current investment decisions; and these will in their turn influence the national income in the future. This conception is the basis for the type of treatment which Mr. Lundberg has called "model sequencies."[1]

Let us consider in each period the average level of investment decisions and the national income. Then the income in, say, period two is a function of investment

[1] *Studies in the Theory of Economic Expansion*, Erik Lundberg, London, 1937. It was applied also in my paper in *Review of Economic Studies*, February 1937, which appeared about the same time.

decisions in period one. Now the income in period two, as we shall see below, determines in conjunction with some other factors the investment decisions in this period, and they in turn the national income in period three, and so on.

So far we have established precisely only the connection between investment decisions and income. Now we shall inquire more closely into the determinants of investment decisions.

THE INDUCEMENT TO INVEST

1. Our argument about the inducement to invest, i.e. about the factors determining investment decisions, is based on some of the results arrived at in the essay on "The Principle of Increasing Risk."

We concluded there that the "commitments" which an entrepreneur is willing to enter at any time are an increasing function of net profitability, i.e. of the difference between the marginal rate of profit and the rate of interest. The same holds good for entrepreneurs as a whole.[1]

"Commitments" were defined as follows:

Commitments = Capital equipment (valued at cost)
    + Investment orders in execution (or just given)
    − Private capital (inclusive of amortization funds)

[1] It is clear that in general the marginal rates of profit in various industries are not equal. But we can define the general marginal rate of profit as such a rate which, if it were to prevail in all industries, would affect the "commitments" in the same way as the given set of marginal rates of profit.

We can now add all such equations relating to individual entrepreneurs, and thus obtain a similar equation for entrepreneurs as a whole.

One may divide outstanding investment orders into the part already produced and the part yet to be completed. If, e.g., one-third of a factory whose total cost of construction is £1,500,000 has already been constructed, the value of the former part is £500,000, and of the latter £1,000,000. The former part is nothing else than capital in the course of construction. Thus the equation of "commitments" may be written as follows:

Commitments = Capital equipment + Capital in the course of construction + The uncompleted part of outstanding orders — Private capital.

or:

Commitments = (Capital equipment + Capital in the course of construction — Private capital) + The uncompleted part of outstanding orders.

It is easy to see that in our model the expression in brackets is constant. Indeed, in a unit of time the sum of capital equipment and capital in the course of construction increases by the value of the output of fixed capital equipment, i.e. by the value of investment. On the other hand, the private capital of entrepreneurs increases by the value of the total saving, for according to our simplifying assumptions entrepreneurs are the only savers in our system. As investment equals saving, the sum of capital equipment and capital in the course of construction minus the private capital of entrepreneurs remains constant through time. Consequently "commitments" vary only because of changes in "the uncompleted part of outstanding investment orders." Thus since "commitments" are an increasing function of the gap between the marginal rate of profit and the rate of interest, the same must also be true of the uncompleted part of investment orders.

However great *actual* investment, i.e. the output of investment goods, may be, it cannot increase aggregate "commitments," for entrepreneurs (being the only savers) must save as a body always just as much as they invest. Thus increasing risk cannot charge "actual investment." The point where it does exert its pressure is on the unexecuted investment decisions. For an investment decision taken, but as yet unexecuted, has no counterpart in saving. And an increase in the uncompleted part of investment decisions—the only way in which aggregate "commitments" may increase in our system—thus requires a higher gap between the rate of profit and the rate of interest.

2. So far we have stated the functional connection between the *stock* of the uncompleted parts of investment orders and the difference between the marginal rate of profit and the rate of interest. Our real aim, however, is to find out what are the determinants of the *rate* of investment decisions. There is obviously a close connection between these two problems. The flow of new investment decisions must be such as to keep the stock

of the uncompleted parts of investment orders at the level corresponding to the prevailing net profitability. Now the period of turnover of this stock is $\frac{\bar{\theta}}{2}$, the time-lag between D (the rate of investment decisions) and I (the output of investment goods). Thus approximately the stock of unexecuted investment orders is equal to $D \cdot \frac{\bar{\theta}}{2}$. It follows that the rate of investment decisions D is also a function of the difference between the prospective rate of profit and the rate of interest.[1]

3. Some readers may regard this discussion about the functional relation between the rate of investment decisions and net profitability as labouring the obvious. This theorem has indeed been often used (more or less implicitly), but so far as I know it has not been satisfactorily demonstrated. To make, e.g., a statement that net profitability is an incentive to invest does not

---

[1] "Commitments" we have considered as measured in terms of money, while D is the *volume* of investment decisions per unit of time. The money value of D is Dp_i where p_i is the index of prices of investment goods. Thus it may seem that it is $Dp_i \cdot \frac{\bar{\theta}}{2}$ and not $D \cdot \frac{\bar{\theta}}{2}$ which is the function of net profitability. While $D \cdot \frac{\bar{\theta}}{2}$ would then be equal to this function divided by the price index p_i. But, e.g., if p_i rises, entrepreneurs are inclined to evaluate their wealth higher and to enter greater commitments. This may be roughly accounted for by assuming not $Dp_i \cdot \frac{\bar{\theta}}{2}$ but $D \cdot \frac{\bar{\theta}}{2}$ to be a function of net profitability.

establish that the *rate* of investment decisions is a function of net profitability.

Further, our argument shows that this theorem holds good only under special assumptions. We assumed in our simplified model that rentiers and workers do not save. If they do, entrepreneurs' "commitments" increase permanently by the amount saved "outside enterprises" (for the saving of entrepreneurs falls short of investment by this amount).

If in an economy the steady accumulation of "non-entrepreneurial" savings is accompanied by a secular growth of wealth the ratio of "commitments" to private capital of enterprises may not rise, and the investment activity may not be impaired by saving "outside enterprises."

If, however, we consider a system having no secular trend, the accumulation of savings "outside enterprises" must cause a "structural slump" of investment activity which is not due to the change in net profitability. For with a given net profitability the rate of investment decisions must decline because otherwise the marginal risk would increase.

This is the reason why, in order to construct a system tending neither to grow nor to shrink in the long run, we assumed the salary earners and rentiers not to save.

TWO DETERMINANTS OF INVESTMENT DECISIONS

1. We have shown that in our system the rate of investment decisions D is an increasing function of the difference between the marginal rate of profit and the

rate of interest. Since it is the long-term rate that matters here, and this was assumed constant, D is an increasing function of the marginal rate of profit. We are now going to show that the marginal rate of profit at a given time—by which is meant the marginal *prospective* rate of profit (see p. 96)—is determined *grosso modo* by the level of the national income Y and the stock of capital equipment. And thus these two factors are together the determinants of the rate of investment decisions. We shall first consider the effect of changes in the national income with a given capital equipment, and afterwards allow for changes in the latter.

2. As follows from the considerations on p. 60, the level of national income Y (expressed in stable values) determines approximately its distribution between various classes. In particular Y determines more or less closely the total capitalists' income Q (expressed in stable values).

Let us denote now by p the index of prices of finished (investment and consumption) goods by which we deflated the money income in order to obtain "income in stable values." The money national income is of course Yp, and total money capitalists' income Qp.

The greater Qp is with a given capital equipment, the greater will be the capitalists' income qp, which can be obtained at present from a given new investment (q is this income expressed in "stable values"). We now denote the index of prices of investment goods by p_i. It is easy to see that the capitalists' income per unit of newly-invested capital is proportionate to $\frac{qp}{p_i}$. But since, according to the result arrived at in the first essay, the prices of finished investment goods vary in approximately the same way as those of finished consumption goods, the ratio $\frac{qp}{p_i}$ is practically equal to q, which with given capital equipment is the greater, the greater is the actual capitalists' income expressed in stable values. And as this latter is determined by the national income Y, it follows that the rate of capitalists' income which can be obtained under current conditions from a new investment is the greater the greater is the national income Y (with a given capital equipment).

The rate of capitalists' income which can be obtained now from a new investment is not a sufficient basis for the estimate of the prospective rate of profit, for future developments must be taken into account. But since conjectures on this subject are extremely vague, present affairs have a predominant influence upon long-term expectations. Knowing so little about the future, entrepreneurs are inclined to be optimists when present trade is good and pessimists when it is bad. Thus as a good approximation we may assume that the rate of profit is a function of q, and thus with given capital equipment is the greater the greater is the national income Y. And since the rate of investment decisions D is an increasing function of the marginal rate of profit we have finally the equation

$$D = \phi_6(Y) \quad . \quad . \quad . \quad . \quad . \quad (14)$$

134

where ϕ is an increasing function and the index e means that it is determined only with a given capital equipment.

3. There are good reasons to believe that the curve representing the function ϕ is S-shaped (see Fig. 11). For when things are improving entrepreneurs become more optimistic about their future, and the rate of investment decisions increases strongly; but after a certain point doubts begin to arise as to the stability of this development, optimism ceases to keep pace with the boom, and the rate of investment decisions tends to increase less rapidly. In the slump a symmetrical development is likely to occur.

The function ϕ represents the dependence of the rate of investment decisions at time t on the national income Y at the same time:

$$D_t = \phi_e(Y_t) \quad . \quad . \quad . \quad . \quad (14a)$$

We have, however, established another connection between these variables; the national income at time t is determined by the rate of investment decisions at time $t - \tau$, where τ is the time-lag depending both on the construction period and on the lag between income and consumption. In other words, the national income at time $t + \tau$ is a function of investment decisions at time t:

$$Y_{t + \tau} = f(D_t) \quad . \quad . \quad . \quad . \quad (13b)$$

Both functions are represented on Fig. 11. The ordinate of the S-shaped ϕ curve shows the rate of investment decisions D_t corresponding to national income Y_t;

while the abscissa of the f-curve (which is taken here to be a straight line[1] corresponding to D_t gives $Y_{t+\tau}$, i.e. the national income at the time $t + \tau$. Owing to the ϕ-curve being S-shaped, it must cut the f-curve in some point B. We shall see at once that from these two curves we can find out how the system moves.

Let us imagine time to be divided into τ periods.

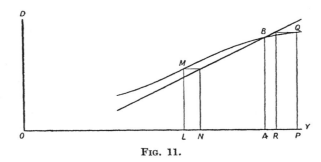

FIG. 11.

Suppose that in an initial τ period the national income has the value OL.

The rate of investment decisions in this period is determined by the ordinate of the ϕ-curve LM. These investment decisions, however, determine in turn the national income in the next τ period, which is equal to the corresponding abscissa of the f-curve ON. Thus the national income is increasing.

On the other hand, if the national income in the initial period has the value OP investment decisions in this period are equal to PQ, and the national income in

---

[1] As we have seen in the first essay, the diagram of the function f for the U.S.A. was a straight line. (See p. 73.)

the next period is OR. Thus the national income is here diminishing.

While if Y is equal to OA, the abscissa of the point of intersection B of the ϕ- and f-curves, the national income tends neither to rise nor to fall.

To sum up: If the point Y, D lies above the f-curve, i.e. if the present investment decisions are higher than investment decisions in the preceding τ period, which have determined the present national income, this increases. If the point Y, D lies below the f-curve, i.e. if the present investment decisions are lower than those which have determined the present national income, this falls off. While if the point Y, D coincides with the point of intersection B of the ϕ- and f-curves, i.e. if the present investment decisions are equal to those which have determined the present national income, this is stationary. Thus the point Y, D either moves towards B, or remains stationary if it coincides with it.

4. A problem concerning the upward movement of the system towards the point B must yet be touched upon.

It is theoretically possible that before point B is reached employment might rise so much as to absorb the total available labour supply. In other words, the abscissa of point B might exceed the level of the national income at which full employment is attained. If, however, there exists at the point of full employment a tendency for a further rise in investment (expressed in stable values), the system must come into a state of

137

"inflation" characterized by a violent rise in wages and prices, while no further increase in the "real" national income can occur.

The "inflation" would eventually be checked by an "automatic" rise in the rate of interest (see p. 115). The rise in wages and prices would cause a strong increase in the short-term rate of interest, and a much smaller but still appreciable one in the long-term rate. Thus

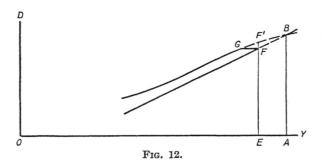

FIG. 12.

under "inflationary" conditions our assumption of a stable long-term rate would not hold good; for under such conditions it would increase until investment activity fell to a level compatible with the existing supply of labour. This may be very clearly represented on our diagram of the ϕ and f functions (Fig. 12). Suppose that full employment is reached at a point E, which lies to the left of point A. In order to prevent inflation, the rate of interest must increase so as to keep the rate of investment decisions at the level EF, for this rate determines the level of the national income equal to OE

138

at which all available labour is absorbed. The rate of investment decisions is *not* equal to EF″ because of the rise in the rate of interest. The rise in the rate of interest as the system approaches full employment causes the curve ϕ, determining the rate of investment decisions in terms of income, to flatten out along GF instead of rising to F″, so that its point of intersection with the *f*-curve is F instead of B. In this way the case when full employment is reached may easily be accounted for in our analysis. We have already indicated, however (p. 115), that such a situation is rather exceptional; thus as a rule point B lies to the left of point F″.

5. B represents a conditional equilibrium in the sense that at this point the system has no tendency to change provided that there is no change in capital equipment (which has so far been assumed constant). However, as investment is generally not at the level of wear and tear, equipment *does* change, and, as will be shown in detail below, the state of "conditional equilibrium" cannot be permanent.

Many writers[1] who have constructed simplified models of the Keynesian theory have focussed their attention on the "equilibrium" represented by the point B. This was due to the fact that they did not distinguish between investment decisions and investment. They were there-

[1] J. E. Meade, "A Simplified Model of Mr. Keynes's System," *Review of Economic Studies*, February 1937.

J. R. Hicks, "Mr. Keynes and the Classics," *Econometrica*, April 1937.

Oskar Lange, "The Rate of Interest and the Optimum Propensity to Consume," *Economica*, February 1938.

fore unable to conceive of the system being in a position different from that presented by the point B.

In addition they did not consider the influence of changes in capital equipment.

It is true that—as shown above—the system always moves towards the point B, but it may, of course, take several τ periods to come close to it. Thus the time of adjustment is considerable (τ is more than half a year).

When at last "equilibrium" is reached, it cannot last long because of the change in capital equipment. Thus the position of "conditional equilibrium" is rather exceptional. As we shall see, it is attained only at the top of the boom and at the bottom of the slump.

6. We have so far examined the dependence of the rate of investment decisions D on the national income Y under the assumption of a given capital equipment. We must now analyse the influence of changes in equipment on investment decisions with a constant national income. In this way we shall be able to describe D as a function of both national income Y and capital equipment.

It is easy to see that if the capacity of equipment increases while Y is stationary, the "state of affairs" becomes worse. Capitalist's income Q (expressed in stable values) is, with constant Y, still approximately constant. Thus the capitalists' income "per factory" must diminish. The new plants compete with the "old" ones, and draw from them a part of the total sales. In this way a part of aggregate profits is transferred to "new" factories.

140

This deterioration in the "state of affairs" clearly influences adversely the prospective rate of profit. Thus we can conclude that the greater the equipment with constant national income the smaller the rate of investment decisions. Consequently the curve representing the function

$$D = \phi_e(Y)$$

is shifted downwards when equipment increases. D is

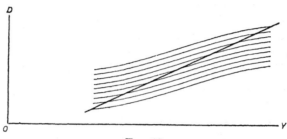

FIG. 13.

in this way a function of two determinants, the national income and capital equipment. It is represented by a family of ϕ_e-curves.

THE BUSINESS CYCLE

1. With the results arrived at in the preceding section, we are now able to describe the dynamic process in our system. The time is supposed to be divided into τ periods. To simplify the exposition, we will examine this process in two stages: in the first we abstract the changes in capital equipment; in the second stage we

141

allow for the effect of these changes which result from investment and wear and tear.[1]

Suppose the level of national income (expressed in stable values) in the first τ period to be Y_1 (see Fig. 13). (4? The corresponding ordinate of the curve ϕ, which represents the dependence of the rate of investment decisions on national income (with given capital equipment), is

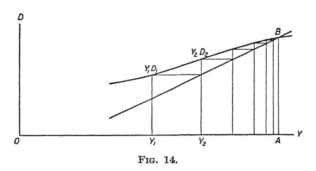

FIG. 14.

the rate of investment decisions D_1, in the first period. In turn D_1 defines the national income Y_2 in the second τ period, which causes in the same period a rate of investment decisions D_2, etc. The point Y, D moves along the ϕ-curve, and, strictly speaking, it never reaches the point B, or, in other words, reaches B only after the lapse of an infinite number of periods. It is clear, however, that after a relatively small number of

[1] In the first stage we can imagine, for instance, that both investment and wear and tear are very small in relation to equipment; thus equipment changes only a little in the course of the process considered.

142

periods the difference between Y, D and Y_B, D_B is negligible, i.e. the position of equilibrium is practically reached. For in succeeding τ periods the increase in Y and D is negligible.

Starting from the position represented by a point Y, D lying above the f-curve we obtain an upward "self-stimulating" process in which D and Y tend to reach the level D_B and Y_B. It is easy to see that if the initial position is represented by a point Y, D, lying below the f-curve, this process is reversed, and the system travels downwards towards B. As already mentioned the position Y_B, D_B is that of equilibrium only on the assumption of a constant equipment. We shall see in the next paragraph that it is the change in equipment which disturbs this equilibrium.

2. We come to the second stage of our argument: we have now to consider the influence exerted upon the dynamic process by changes in the capacity of equipment.

To every state of capital equipment there corresponds a certain level of investment necessary for the maintenance of its capacity, i.e. to make good wear and tear.

If the upward self-stimulating process described in the preceding paragraph starts from a position in which deliveries of investment goods are lower than the "level of maintenance," so that capacity is shrinking, the rise of investment is thereby stimulated. The ϕ-curve, up which the point Y, D moves, itself shifts upwards. But the situation alters when the deliveries of investment goods begin to exceed the level of maintenance. From

143

then onwards capital equipment keeps expanding, and the upward process is retarded. The point Y, D moves farther up the ϕ-curve, but now the latter shifts downwards. Similarly a downward "self-stimulating" process (which is represented by a downward movement of the point Y, D along the ϕ-curve) is initially strengthened by the expansion of capital equipment, but afterwards hampered by its shrinkage. The point of intersection of the ϕ- and f-curves B is now *not* a position of equilibrium. If investment decisions D_B are greater than the maintenance level of equipment, so also will be the deliveries of investment goods; thus capital equipment will increase and the ϕ-curve shift downwards. If D_B is less than the "maintenance level" the reverse must occur.

We shall see in the next paragraph that the "self-stimulating process" (represented by the movement of point Y, D along the ϕ-curve), and the change in the capital equipment (represented by the shift of the ϕ-curve), create together an automatic business cycle.

3. Imagine that in the initial position income and investment decisions are represented by the point E in the Y, D plane (Fig. 15), and that at this point the deliveries of investment goods are just equal to the maintenance level of equipment. Thus as equipment is neither expanding nor shrinking, the ϕ-curve is stationary in the period considered. The point Y, D tends to move up this curve, but in succeeding periods investment activity increases, and the ϕ-curve shifts downwards. As a result the moving point Y, D has the

trajectory EF, which is the resultant of its movement up the downward shifting ϕ-curve. (At E this trajectory is tangential to the ϕ-curve, since Y, D is there moving along ϕ while the latter is stationary.) After point F, in which the national income Y ceases to grow, has been reached, the ϕ-curve still shifts downwards, consequently point Y, D moves vertically downwards. Thus it

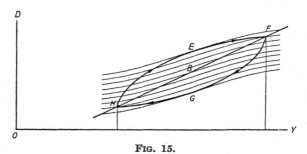

FIG. 15.

The cracs of the curve EFGH in F and H are due to the discontinuity introduced by division of the process into τ periods.

falls below the f-curve and begins to move down the ϕ-curve, which itself shifts downwards because investment activity still exceeds the maintenance level of capital equipment. But after a certain time the steady fall in investment decisions brings the system to the position G, in which deliveries of investment goods just cover wear and tear. The ϕ-curve now ceases to shift downwards, and the trajectory becomes tangential to it, as it was before in E. In succeeding periods investment activity is lower than the level of main-

145   K

tenance, so that the ϕ-curve begins to shift upwards, but as the point Y, D is still below the f-curve, it continues to move down the ϕ-curve. At point H income Y ceases to fall, while the ϕ-curve continues to shift upwards. Consequently point Y, D rises vertically. As the point Y, D comes in this way above the f-curve its movement along the ϕ-curve is now upward, while ϕ-curve itself continues to shift upwards. Thus the moving point comes back to point E and a new cycle begins.

We now see clearly that a business cycle is inherent in our model. This may be summarized shortly as follows:

4. We start from a position in which the requirements of wear and tear are just covered by investment activity, and in which investment decisions are at such a level that they tend to cause a higher level of income in the future (point E). Thus equipment is initially stationary while national income tends to rise. The result is a further rise in investment decisions, and later in income, and so on cumulatively. However, capital equipment also expands, because investment activity increases above the level of maintenance. This hampers the "self-stimulating" process of the rise in investment decisions and national income. After a certain time a position is reached in which national income ceases to grow (point F). But investment activity, which is now at its maximum, continues to add to the stock of capital equipment. Income being stationary, this brings the first fall in investment decisions, and thus breaks the boom. The fall of investment decisions causes a fall in

146

income, which in turn depresses investment decisions. So long as investment activity is higher than the level of maintenance, the downward movement is aggravated by the continued expansion of capital equipment. The effect of the latter is reversed when investment activity falls below the level of wear and tear (point G), i.e. capital equipment shrinks, and thus hampers the downward movement. Eventually the position is reached at which national income ceases to fall (point H). The shrinkage of capital equipment continues, however, and, as income is stationary, this starts a rise in investment decisions. Thus the bottom of the slump is passed. The rise in investment decisions causes a rise in income, which in turn further stimulates investment decisions. This upward process is accelerated by the shrinkage of capital equipment until investment activity reaches the level of maintenance (point E), and a new cycle begins.

5. We are now going back for a moment to our diagram. It is clear that the moving point cannot stop anywhere on the trajectory. At E and G equipment is stationary, but investment decisions are such as to cause in the next period a level of income which is higher or lower respectively than the present one, and thus to start a "self-stimulating" process. At F and H there is no tendency for "self-stimulating" process, but the amount of equipment is changing. There exists, however, on the f-curve somewhere between F and H a point B, at which investment activity just covers wear and tear. This point corresponds to a long-run equilibrium. For since it lies on the f-curve there is no tendency for a

147

self-stimulating process to begin; investment decisions, and therefore deliveries of finished investment goods, tend to be stable; while since they are both at the level of maintenance there is no change in equipment. If in its initial position the moving point does not coincide with B, it must move around B, and a business cycle arises.[1]

6. We see that the question, "What causes periodical crises?" could be answered shortly: the fact that investment is not only produced but also producing. Investment considered as expenditure is the source of prosperity, and every increase of it improves business and stimulates a further rise of investment. But at the same time every investment is an addition to capital equipment, and right from birth it competes with the older

[1] Clearly it is an arbitrary and even unlikely assumption that the moving point comes back to its initial position E—the trajectory may well be a spiral and not a closed curve. If the fluctuations produced by our mechanism have a tendency to subside, this means that the spiral converges towards point B, and in this way the system tends to attain long-run equilibrium. But as shown by the investigations of Professor Frisch ("Propagation problem and impulse problems in dynamics," *Economic Essays in honour of Gustav Cassel*, London, 1933, and unpublished works), this is prevented by the existence of "erratic shocks." Since the relationships represented by f and ϕ are in reality not quite stable functions, the actual dynamic process may be imagined as the resultant of the operation of the mechanism described above and of random shocks. Now Professor Frisch has shown that if the basic mechanism produces slightly damped fluctuations the existence of shocks establishes a state of relatively regular undamped fluctuations with an average period similar to that of the fluctuations created by the "basic mechanism."

generation of this equipment. The tragedy of investment is that it causes crisis because it is useful. Doubtless many people will consider this theory paradoxical. But it is not the theory which is paradoxical, but its subject —the capitalist economy.

INDEX

STATISTICAL INDEX

(Numbers refer to numbers of tables)

Printed in Great Britain
by Amazon.co.uk, Ltd.,
Marston Gate.